SHAVING

THE INSIDE

OF YOUR SKULL

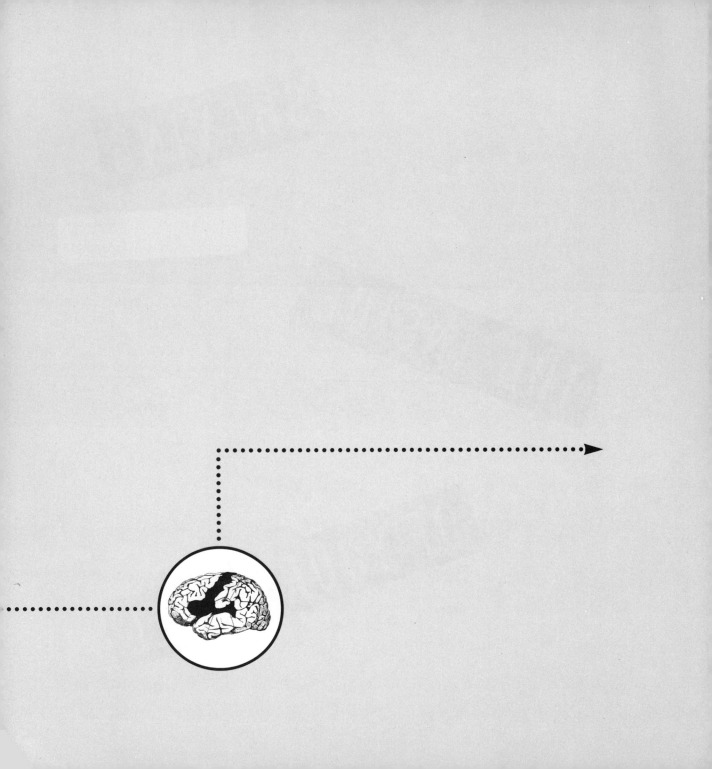

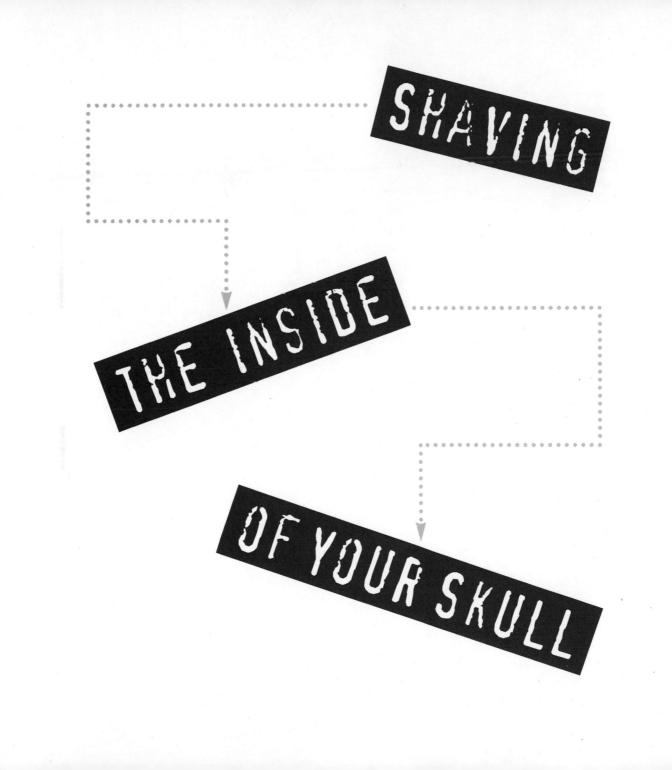

Also by the author

The Zen of Recovery
Beat Spirit (forthcoming)

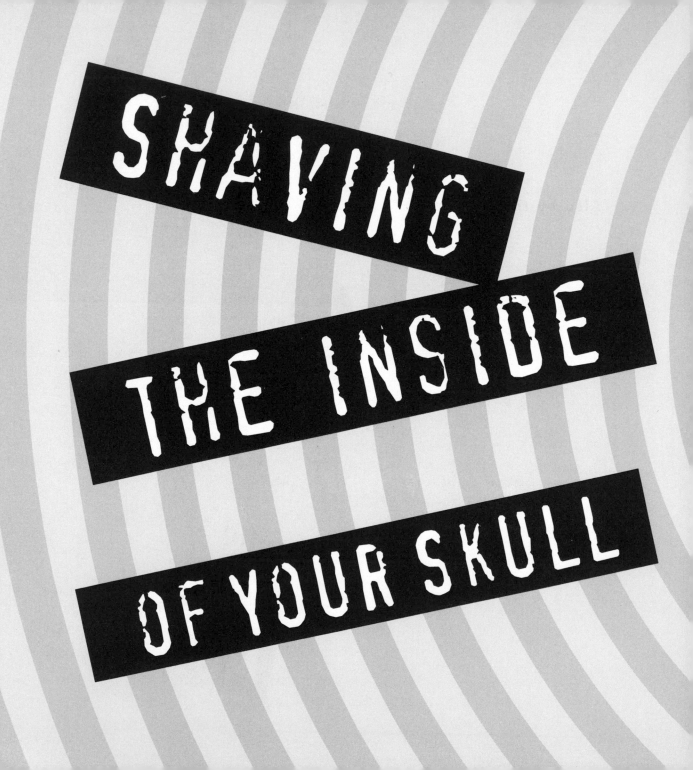

INTRODUCTION

Zen monks

have traditionally shaven their heads as a symbol of their renunciation of the world, its desires and ways. Beat poet and Zen student Lew Welch said it wasn't enough to merely shave the outside of your head if you hadn't shaved the inside as well. All too often, we confuse the exterior fashions and symbols of belief with true interior change.

Shaving the inside of your skull is the same as pulling out the weeds of dry and dead belief that threaten to choke your potential and freedom. It's as simple as realizing that there is something growing inside your skull as well as outside, and that while you may not have planted it there, you are fertilizing it with your fears, guilt, and anger.

Shaving the inside of your skull and eliminating the need for the crutches of belief and "isms" will make a bigger difference for you and the world than a haircut or mere change of beliefs ever did. Abbie Hoffman insisted that all our limiting "-isms" become "-wasms."

There is nothing inherently wrong with holding beliefs. There is something very wrong when the belief holds us. How can we learn to know the difference?

This book is about shaving the inside of our skulls, about identifying and getting rid of the dense growth of beliefs, imprinting, and concepts inside our heads that cause us pain and keep us asleep. Once our skulls are emptied of the tangled and choking growth of belief and expectation, all things become possible and flow unimpeded through our spacious heads and spirits.

Our skulls and spirits should be vast and empty caverns of delight through which pass the winds of life, not dark and drear places where we fearfully huddle amidst the piles of spiritual and emotional debris that we call our own.

WE'VE BEEN LIED TO ALL OUR LIVES!

We've been sold the sizzle and not the steak, the bark and not the bite. We've been put up for auction and down for the count. We've been taken for granted and just flat out taken.

We've been kept in the dark, told to lighten up, sent to the back, and given a false front. We've been taught to pull the wool over our own eyes and call it vision.

We've been lied to all our lives!

What are we waiting for? A UPC bar code to be tattooed on our foreheads? Our beliefs thereby easily scanned and identified as "normal"? Our beliefs are driving us crazy. They're not even "our" beliefs! "Our" beliefs are keeping us from becoming *who we really are.*

SPIRITUAL COURAGE

If the book we are reading does not wake us, as with a fist hammering on our skull, why then do we read it? A book must be an ice-axe to break the sea frozen inside us.

—Franz Kafka

Most experts today would tell you that the problem with the world is that people don't have anything to believe in. This is ridiculous; in fact, the problem with the world is *too many* beliefs and too many easy things to believe in. Beliefs are often the refuge of the coward.

To confront life *as it is,* without beliefs, is the mark of real spiritual and human courage. Or as Alan Watts liked to describe himself, being "unrutted" in our beliefs and ways of being becomes the most creative and fulfilling way to live.

We really don't have to do anything as radical as shaving the outsides of our heads, entering monasteries, or taking vows. Right here and right now is the place in which we can wake up and resume our human lives, reclaimed as truly our own, not subject to the manipulative anxieties of advertising, the demeaning divisions of politics,

A User's Guide to Psyche, Self & Transformation

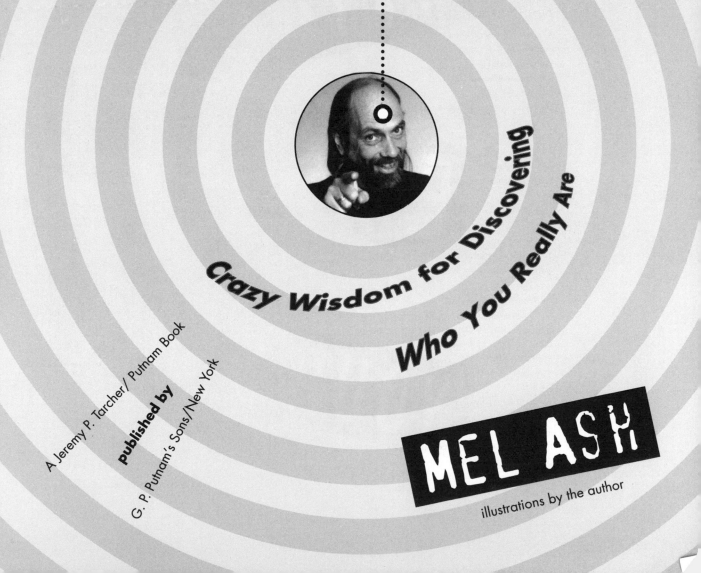

Crazy Wisdom for Discovering

Who You Really Are

A Jeremy P. Tarcher/ Putnam Book

published by

G. P. Putnam's Sons/New York

MEL ASH

illustrations by the author

Most Tarcher/Putnam books are available at special quantity discounts for bulk purchases for sales promotions, premiums, fund-raising, and educational needs. Special books or book excerpts also can be created to fit specific needs. For details, write or telephone Special Markets, The Putnam Publishing Group, 200 Madison Ave., New York, NY 10016; (212) 951-8891.

. . . .

A Jeremy P. Tarcher/Putnam Book
Published by G. P. Putnam's Sons
Publishers Since 1838
200 Madison Avenue
New York, NY 10016
http://www. putnam.com/putnam

Library of Congress Cataloging-in-Publication Data
Ash, Mel.
Shaving the inside of your skull : crazy wisdom for discovering who you really are : a user's guide to psyche, self & transformation / by Mel Ash.
p.   cm.
ISBN 0-87477-841-7
1. Self-perception.   2. Self-evaluation.
3. Introspection.   4. Change (Psychology)
I. Title.
BF697.5.S43A84   1997   96-20618   CIP
158—dc20

Design by JUDITH STAGNITTO ABBATE
Cover design by MEL ASH
Cover collage and painting © *1996 by* ELEANOR ASH
Photograph of the author © *1996 by* PETER GOLDBERG
Printed in the United States of America
1   2   3   4   5   6   7   8   9   10
This book is printed on acid-free paper. ∞

For Eleanor, Aren, and Ethan,

who know the inside of my skull better than anyone,

and

Rev. Tom Ahlburn,

who keeps the razors sharp.

ACKNOWLEDGMENTS

Thanks and a tip o' the skull to:

Jeremy Tarcher, spiritual and psychological rebbe and roshi for many of us, knowingly or not, in deep gratitude for his advocacy of transformative vision and his belief in those who struggle to realize its probability; who I am and what this book represents owe much to the Tarcher tradition;

Sarah-la Owens-Ash, my split-apart, fearless partner in transcending limits and goddess of the eastern seaboard airwaves, whose unconditional love saw this book and its author through to the end, for her collaboration and original concepts for the many illustrations;

Alan Rinzler, editor extraordinaire, for challenging me at every turn to live up to the promise of the text and make it worthy of the lineage it represents; Robert Welsch, who helped guide and shape this book with his willingness to stretch both our limits; David Groff, my final editor, taskmaster, and cheerleader, who shepherded this book to completion with sympathy and style; Timothy Meyer, for his superb copyediting; the production and design team of Tricia Martin, Diane Lomonaco, and Claire Vaccaro; Judith Stagnitto Abbate, for her amazing book design and revolutionary graphic collaboration; PR guru Ken Siman; and Irene Prokop, who put up with me and all of the above in making this vision a reality;

Barbara Lowenstein, for her ongoing support of my work, and to the capable people in her office: Elise Proulx and Norman Kurz;

Also to: Alison Meyers, legendary bookseller bodhisattva, cultural worker, editor, sister, muse, and inspiration for much of the spirit of this book and the catalyst for who I am becoming; Ann Patrick, fellow writer, for being a constant and dependable presence all these years at every level I can imagine; the fearless members of First Unitarian of Providence for nurturing this work and providing a willing laboratory; Tim "Neutrix" Martin, mindfulness teacher, whose consternations keep me balanced, also for his talents as a hand and epiglottis model; Eleanor Ash, for her wonderful cover design; Kay Pascalides, Ruth Ahlburn, Frank and Betty Reed, Rev. Neil Bakker, Daniel Malvin, Peter Goldberg; Georgiana and Joe Owens, Frank Difficult, Newspeak Books, Obsidian Video, In Your Ear Records; Cellar Stories; Charles Dexter Ward for the use of his magnificent and arcane library, Zen Blues Master Maynard Silva, Ray Haaker, Rev. David Proctor, the Ash women: Beth, Amy, Karin, Hannah, Melanie, and Laura; Chris Denslow, the Learning Connection of Providence; Deb and Judy of First Class in Washington, D.C., Open Center, Interface, Rowe Camp and Conference Center; music from: Axiom, the Robert Jazz Quartet, Jason Kendall and the Amazing Royal Crowns, and "Vampyros Lesbos"; the sacred memory of Everyday Books; the many people who've read my first book and attended my workshops around the country; the living legacy of Timothy Leary (he's looking in) and, as always, Scott Rundlett.

CONTENTS

 Introduction 1

 How to Begin Shaving the Inside of Your Skull

 Checklist for Shaving the Inside of Your Skull

First Shave: Who We're Supposed to Be
At the Scene of the Accident / **29**
Define Normyl / **35**
First Set of Razors / **47**

 Second Shave: Who We're Told to Be
I Like What I Know and I Know What I Like / **71**
The Construction of Consciousness / **79**
Second Set of Razors / **85**

Third Shave: Who We Think We Are

Shrinking Your Own Head / **103**
Do-It-Yourself Brain Surgery / **113**
Third Set of Razors / **123**

Fourth Shave: Who We Might Become

Beyond Belief / **147**
The Meaning of Life / **155**
Fourth Set of Razors / **161**

Fifth Shave: Who We Really Are

Revolt! / **185**
Fifth Set of Razors / **193**

Reading Razors

The Two Commandments of Belief / **217**
About the Author / **219**

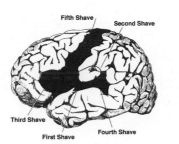

Fifth Shave | Second Shave
Third Shave
First Shave | Fourth Shave

Society everywhere is in conspiracy
against every one of its members.
The virtue in most request is conformity.
Self-reliance is its aversion.
One who would gather immortal palms
must not be hindered by the name of goodness,
but must explore if it be goodness.
Nothing is at last sacred
but the integrity of your own mind.

—Ralph Waldo Emerson

Limits are beliefs to be transcended.

—Dr. John Lilly

If the mind depends upon anything,
it has no sure haven.

—Buddha

and the degrading admonitions of religion. The work of becoming *who you really are* needn't be exotic or esoteric. It's very simple and everyday.

This book is not selling any agenda, belief, or system. Whatever you are, whoever you are, wherever you are, become only that, be only there. Unrut yourself. Use whatever is at hand to get the job done. Do not make new gods or beliefs out of your new tools for transformation. Let them go when their time has come.

WHO WE REALLY ARE

Our true, deeper selves demand transcendence and transformation of false, limited being. We begin to become who we were supposed to be all along: ourselves, or what both Asian and Native American traditions call "real human beings"; nothing more, nothing less, at home in both our skins and the world.

The limits to our awakening and happiness are only those that we choose to believe. Jewish mystics teach that each of us is something completely unique in this universe, absolutely necessary parts of the greater pattern. They teach that universal enlightenment and peace will not come until that day when each one of us is completely and uniquely ourselves, freed of the beliefs that cause us to live other people's lives, think other people's thoughts, and even die other people's deaths.

We vainly believe that by changing beliefs and their symbols, shaving the outsides of our skulls, if you will, we are somehow changed and become real. We know from hard experience that this is not the case. Our new beliefs only become more fashionable forms of mental slavery and spiritual numbness.

Nobody believes that there's nothing to believe in.

—Jack Kerouac

RISKS AND SHAVING THE INSIDE OF YOUR SKULL

Just as we cannot immediately relax our tense muscles but must consciously massage them into a state of openness, so, too, is the work of returning to our original state through the deliberate courting of transformative experiences. It might even feel uncomfortable, risky, and alien at first. But we must take these as signs of progress and awakening, not as an excuse to return to the familiar prison of small self, of *who we're told to be.*

Shaving the inside of our skulls is a work that demands a confrontation with ourselves, rather than searching outside for scapegoats or saviors. It is an expansion of limits through deliberate risk-taking and a relentless questioning of what constitutes "normal."

Shaving the inside of our skulls is the self-directed process by which we literally remove the limits to our potential by testing, stretching, and examining *who we're supposed to be, who we were told to be,* and *who we think we are.* Every question asked, every risk taken, and every new experience sought after is a small but necessary step toward becoming *who we really are.*

Most systems of belief will leave you feeling somewhat transformed and secure, perhaps with a warm and fuzzy feeling of fulfillment, even smugness. We might even become better "adjusted"; somewhat happier and better people for a time. But all these thing are mere adjustments really, much like a 100,000-mile tune-up.

The spiritual wear and emotional tear of the days and years soon find us again in the garages of religion and therapy, or seeking better tools and mechanics on bookstore racks or in workshop catalogs. Again, we turn to the panacea of belief and limitation as the only sure cure.

It is by freeing the mind from external influences, whether casual or emotional, that it obtains power to see somewhat of the truth of things.

—Aleister Crowley

PERSONAL AND GLOBAL CONVERGENCE

A couple of analogies come to mind as I attempt to describe what *Shaving the Inside of Your Skull* represents.

First is the rapidly converging global culture and economy. For the first time in history, everything is available to us: languages, literature, myth, commerce. In short, what was previously provincial private property has become our common inheritance. Out of the many: one.

Second: Our information technology is converging in a similar, if faster, fashion. Very soon, most technologies (phone, computer, T.V., CD player, fax, etc.) will be unified into a single unit. Formerly separately functioning entities again become one and, just like global cultures in convergence, are shown to be less dissimilar than thought. Out of the confusion: clarity.

What does all this have to do with this book? Simple. For generations, religion, science, the arts, and other intellectual and spiritual pursuits have all been at odds as they attempt to put their spin on the universe. Each claimed sole possession of the truth of human existence.

Just as in the global and technological convergence, it is becoming apparent that these disciplines are all equally valid and necessary parts of a single machine; that the biologist's brain research might be as spiritually revealing as a poet's haiku, that the videographer's art might be as transformative as a rebbe's parable.

These are different *styles* of approaching the mystery, in the same way that fax and phone, Japanese etiquette and American glad-handing, are branches on the same tree.

This book is therefore a multi-disciplinary and syncretic approach, using whatever fits to make its point. No distinctions are made between thousand-year-old Hindu wisdom and the latest findings of quantum physics, no hierarchy is established between punk rock and the American Revolution, no difference is postulated between spirituality and the

Our heads are round so that our thoughts can fly in any direction.

—Francis Picabia

Our goal is to discover that we have always been where we ought to be.

—Aldous Huxley

electricity in our nervous systems, no political correctness established at the expense of psychedelic research or the methods of Twelve Step programs.

NO ESCAPE FROM THE REAL WORLD

Likewise, no effort is made to draw distinctions between discussions and implications of spirituality, politics, economics, and other formerly walled-off approaches. These realms, as well, interpenetrate and affect each other far more than we acknowledge.

Who we vote for, what we buy, how we worship, all these things impact upon the totality of our deepest beings and are intimately linked. We must engage ourselves and the world on *all* levels when we begin the work of transformation. *Who we really are* is to be found in all areas of life.

GOALS OF THE WORK

The exercises and ideas in this book aim to expand our sense of self into previously undreamed of realms and expand our normally limited consciousness into the larger self that we confuse with system and belief.

The methods seek to remove these beliefs that limit us insofar as our abilities to:

1) fully accept and love ourselves *as we really are;*

2) fully accept the probability that we can consciously transform into *who we really are;*

3) reclaim the dignity and authenticity of our own questions; and

4) become free of the need to attain definitive, compartmentalized answers to life's quandaries.

They lied to you, sold you ideas of good and evil, gave you distrust of your body and shame for your prophethood of chaos, invented words of disgust for your molecular love, mesmerized you with inattention, bored you with civilization.

—Hakim Bey

You're only as young as the last time you changed your mind.

—Timothy Leary

In practicing these methods, one will inevitably become:

1) more spontaneous and creative in both solutions and style;

2) more flexible when dealing with life, learning to flow with the waters of reality rather than getting hung up on the rocks of belief;

3) less needy for external approval, either through material goods or adherence to systems; and

4) less conforming, less fearful, and a whole lot more alive.

Many of the methods in this spiritual work are drawn from spiritual traditions and masters throughout history. I have assembled others from disciplines of psychology, art movements, poetry, novels, and popular music. Still others are of my own creation, ones that have proven effective for me and others.

SPIRITUAL MECHANICS

The exercises, or razors, all aim toward facilitating transformative experiences, ones that will give you new vistas of self and help in the work of shaving the inside of your skull. In all cases, they will bring you face-to-face with the limitations inherent to individual, belief-based consciousness and suggest ways of transcending these limits.

Have I, your author, tried them all out on the laboratory of myself? Yes. You have my personal Underwriters Consciousness Laboratory Seal of Approval on each of them, at great risk and expense to myself.

The methods and ideas have also been extensively researched in numerous workshops throughout the country with hundreds of people just like yourself. Will all these methods work for you? Of course not. But try your best. In the words of Lao-tzu, "The journey of a thousand miles begins with a single step."

> Some people can be reasoned into sense, and others must be shocked into it.
>
> —Thomas Paine

> Whenever I draw a circle, I immediately want to step out of it.
>
> —R. Buckminster Fuller

SELF-CONSCIOUSNESS

As you use these razors, you will surely feel extremely self-conscious, and perhaps even frightened. Persevere! To become *self* conscious is the *goal* of the exercises, to force yourself to stand out in stark relief to your surroundings and more comforting habits.

To become truly self-conscious is to begin to wake up, and it will feel every bit as uncomfortable and strange. Don't succumb to the drowsy inclination to pull the warm blankets of belief back over your true self. Will you feel foolish? Often. Will you feel more alive? Frighteningly so. You will become aware that you have choices in your life you never dreamed possible. Make them.

The razors are, for the most part, free and easy, requiring no surrender of self to outside authorities or priesthoods. You are free to change, alter, and modify them to your heart's content as you change and modify yourself (hopefully, as well, to your heart's everlasting content).

If all goes well, you will have shaved the inside of your skull and recaptured awe, delight, spontaneity, and constant uncritical attention to your life, throwing away all scripts and harmful life-denying beliefs that injure you, others, and the planet. Hopefully, you will begin to experience for yourself the goals set forth by Walt Whitman in his "Song of Myself":

You shall possess the good of the earth and sun . . .
　　there are millions of suns left,
You shall no longer take things at second or third hand . . .
　　nor look through the eyes of the dead . . .
　　nor feed on the spectres in books,
You shall not look through my eyes either, nor take things from me,
You shall listen to all sides and filter them from yourself.

In doing so, you will laugh at the biggest joke ever played on you: your "self." Have a good laugh. Any attempt to explain our lives through beliefs or words is just so much hot air and wind.

These methods and musings are your sails as you embark on your voyage to freedom. The wind is particularly strong and warm right now. The ocean of self and love is safer and larger than we've been told. Its horizons are yours alone to map.

Sail away.

Sail away . . .

Mel Ash
Providence, Rhode Island
Year of the Rat

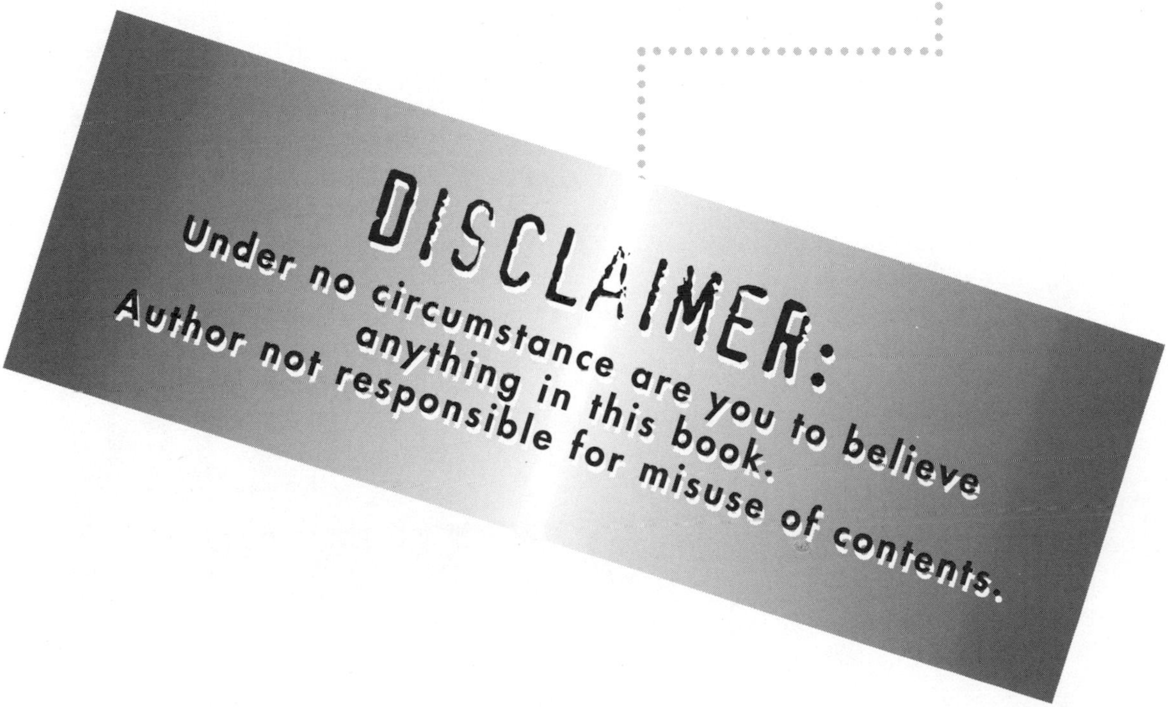

DISCLAIMER:
Under no circumstance are you to believe anything in this book.
Author not responsible for misuse of contents.

Adventure without risk is
Disneyland.

—Douglas Coupland

Do what you will, this life's a
fiction/And is made up of
contradiction.

—William Blake

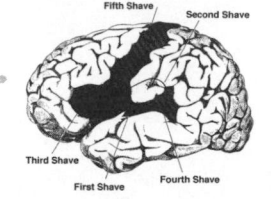

HOW TO BEGIN
SHAVING THE INSIDE OF YOUR SKULL

Structure of the Book

Shaving the Inside of Your Skull is divided into five sections or "Shaves." Each Shave is comprised of essays followed by a set of activities and exercises called "razors."

This is by no means a rigid or easily defined "system." In fact, any attempt to pigeonhole exercises or ideas as "this" or "that" is a violation of the book's intent. Nevertheless, the broad generalizations and organization I have used should at least make the journey a bit more comprehensible and rewarding.

The Essays

The essays examine, in a general way, the theme of each shave, such as the introductory "Who We're Supposed to Be." The exercises, or "razors," in each section are also generally grouped around the section's stated theme, providing you with opportunities to actually implement some of the essay's ideas and challenges.

When reading the essays, bear in mind that they're the product of *my* experience. They are meant to provoke, prod, and make you ponder. They will provide no definitive answers and only seek to make you ask better questions. Feel free to agree or disagree. In fact, you could write your objections or agreements in the margins of the book as one of your razors. This book is about who *you* really are. Try to be that person as you read. Believe nothing. Be open to everything.

The Razors

The razors are literally the tools with which we can shave the insides of our skulls, providing real-life ways to take risks and examine ourselves through new and often challenging experiences.

The razors will generally reflect each Shave's theme. Where they do not, it's because they weren't easily categorized and could really have gone anywhere, but are valuable methods nonetheless and applicable to the work in general. Hence:

SHAVING THE INSIDE OF YOUR SKULL'S

ALL-PURPOSE METHOD

FOR DISTINGUISHING BETWEEN GOOD AND BAD:

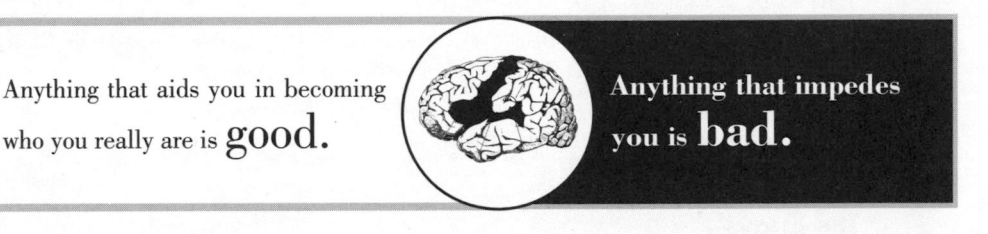

Anything that aids you in becoming who you really are is good.

Anything that impedes you is bad.

The razors are your vehicles for transformation. They are meant to be used. They are not literary exercises to be passively admired or chuckled over. Please make an earnest attempt to try them out. Kick their tires. Drive them around the block. Hell, I don't care . . . take them for joy rides, go as fast or slow as you like. It's your ride. Just try them out, OK?

Journal and Workbook

Many of the razors ask you to do some writing exercises or artwork. It would be helpful for you to get a blank notebook to keep along with your copy of *Shaving the Inside of Your Skull*. You've already purchased this book, so treat yourself to a nice-looking companion blank book that will beckon and invite you to participate. Use it only for discovering *who you really are*.

In addition to filling it with your written and artistic razor exercises, you should also use it as a journal, jotting down your reactions to the razors that don't call for writing. Also record your reflections and discoveries as you shave the inside of your skull, using the journal as a diary of transformation.

I hate and renounce as a coward every being who consents to live without first having re-created himself.

—Antonin Artaud

Suggested Shaving Schedules

Should you do all the razors consecutively and all at once before moving onto the next Shave? Good question! This is, again, not a "one-size-fits-all" system or book. Take what you need and leave the rest. Skip around. Open the book at random.

Consider this book a very extensive and unique menu for all tastes and diets. But if you really want some instructions, here are some ways to order, some serious and some tongue-in-cheek:

1) **Five-day program:** Read a Shave Level per day, essays in the morning. Throughout the day, do as many or few razors as appropriate. Repeat this process throughout the week with succeeding levels.

2) **Five-week program:** Read a Level per week, the essays perhaps on Sunday. Assign yourself a comfortable number of razors per day. Repeat each remaining week with the following levels.

Chew, don't swallow.

—Swami Sarvagatananda, Providence, Rhode Island, regarding beliefs

3) **Five-month program:** Read the essays at the beginning of the month. Assign yourself a reasonable number of razors per week. Repeat each month as indicated.

4) **Five-year program:** You've got plenty of time! Figure out your own schedule as one of your first razors.

5) **Five-decade program:** This is the schedule most people unconsciously and inevitably follow as they evolve and age through the years. Or in other words: Get born. Go along to get along. Maybe you'll learn something. Maybe you won't. All of a sudden, it's over! That's the general plan most follow.

If you choose this method, you don't even have to read this book. Lucky for you it's so nicely designed. It'll look great on your coffee table!

Many of the razors recommend group or couple participation. Those that do not can be easily adapted for two or more people. Any transformative work can be made more effective if you do it with others.

The author suggests numbers 2 and 3 as the most effective and realistic schedules. Or just do it your way, which is really the point of this entire work.

Further Readings as Razors

The reading list at the end of the book is a selection chosen to augment and further the intent of *Shaving the Inside of Your Skull.* Here, once more, I have divided the entries into five sections, corresponding to the Shaves undertaken.

If you are interested in pursuing more information about a specific Shave you are working on, this will provide an easy reference. You could also read some of the recommended selections in conjunction with your work at that Shave, thus rounding out a fully integrated curriculum, complete with "academic" and experiential resources.

Expectations and Results

Will you, at the end of the book, have attained "cosmic consciousness," freedom from limiting beliefs, shaved the inside of your skull and live happily ever? Like all answers, this one contains good news and bad news.

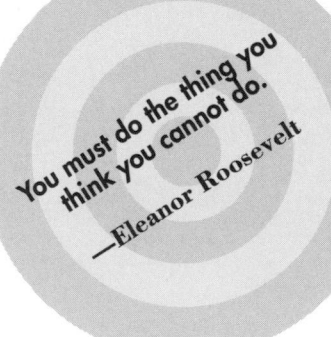

Believe those who are seeking the truth; doubt those who find it.
—André Gide

You must do the thing you think you cannot do.
—Eleanor Roosevelt

The bad news first:

No. This is an artificial and self-conscious "system" designed by another limited human mind only to encourage you to seek your own freedom and to control your *own* destiny. This is in no way an infallible system designed to bring about regularly predictable results. Please transcend and shave even this book.

Now for the good news:

Whatever results you get out of this depend solely upon the amount of effort and attention you put into it. In fact, the less expectation of results you bring to the work, paradoxically, the more you'll actually benefit. After all, much of this book is a thinly veiled argument in favor of surrendering our beliefs about change, results, and expectations.

Just do it for the sheer joy, novelty, and challenge of doing it. Let go of any ideas of "improvement" or "change." You are already *who you are*, moving in the direction you should, like it or not. This book will merely accentuate that process. No guarantees. No graduation ceremony. No completion of this work. Also no beginning. Above all else: Have fun!

> Until we lose ourselves there is no hope of finding ourselves.
>
> —Henry Miller

Trying to define yourself is like trying to bite your own teeth.

—Alan Watts

Self is the barrier against which the world throws itself. Spirit is the wall against which we batter out our poor brains.

—Kenneth Patchen

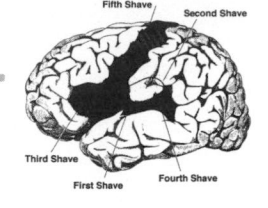

Fifth Shave
Second Shave
Third Shave
First Shave
Fourth Shave

CHECKLIST FOR
SHAVING THE INSIDE OF YOUR SKULL

Here's a list of many of the things we'll be examining throughout this book: the personal beliefs that act as limits and keep us from becoming *who we really are.* It is an arbitrary and incomplete list. There are as many ways of limitation, it seems, as there are people, so I have provided three spaces at the end of each category for you to add your own. You will probably want to make up your own categories as well.

As you read the list, check off the ones that apply to you personally as honestly as you can. Keep them in mind as you read and work the rest of this book. You'll probably even find yourself checking off contradictory answers in the same category. The descriptions you check off indicate some of the stuff inside your skull that we'll be attempting to shave later on.

It is important to always keep in mind that there are no "right" answers or "better" beliefs in this list, so don't feel smug (or unworthy) when considering them. While some beliefs may tend to hasten personal evolution and transformation, that in no way implies their "superiority." All these beliefs are relative, and even the very best of them remain limits that must be transcended.

There's nothing cute like a scoring system to pigeonhole your choices from this list into a "personality type." Its purpose is only to set up the personal discovery program you wish to pursue as you read.

Beliefs about God

- [ ] God exists.
- [ ] God does not exist.
- [ ] God is dead.
- [ ] God is utterly indifferent. (Kurt Vonnegut)
- [ ] God is dog spelled backwards.
- [ ] Dog is God spelled backwards.
- [ ] God? She's black! (Gregory Corso)
- [ ] God is an insane space alien.
- [ ] I am God.
- [ ] We are all God.
- [ ] God is out there in heaven.
- [ ] God is in here in everything.
- [ ] God is a jealous and wrathful god.
- [ ] God is a forgiving and loving god.
- [ ] God is a concept by which we measure our pain. (Lennon)
- [ ] I can know about God.
- [ ] Others must tell me about God.
- [ ] My god can beat up your god.
- [ ] Any god will do.
- [ ] Haven't considered it.
- [ ] Don't know.
- [ ]
- [ ]
- [ ]

Beliefs about Self

- [ ] I am God.
- [ ] I am worthless.
- [ ] I am.
- [ ] I am not.
- [ ] The world owes me.
- [ ] I don't deserve anything.
- [ ] I am a success.
- [ ] I am a failure.
- [ ] I am for real.
- [ ] I am a fake.
- [ ] I am evil.
- [ ] I am good.
- [ ] I can change my life.
- [ ] I am at the hands of fate.
- [ ] I love myself and body.
- [ ] I hate myself and body.
- [ ]
- [ ]
- [ ]

Beliefs about Others

- ☐ Others are more important than me.
- ☐ I am better than others.
- ☐ I'm better than no one and no one is better than me. (Bob Dylan)
- ☐ Go along to get along.
- ☐ Be yourself.
- ☐ Follow the crowd.
- ☐ The majority is always right.
- ☐ Individuals make the difference.
- ☐ My self-image is determined by the opinions of others.
- ☐ My self-image is reliant on my own self-realization.
- ☐ Others are always right.
- ☐ Others shouldn't be upset by me.
- ☐ Others are a threat and a competition to me.
- ☐ Dog eat dog.
- ☐ Others complete me.
- ☐ Cooperation with others is the highest goal.
- ☐ Success is determined by others and exteriors.
- ☐ Success is made in me.
- ☐
- ☐
- ☐

Beliefs about Groups

- ☐ My religion, country, politics, ethnic group . . . is the best and the only right way.
- ☐ My . . . is one among many; a style of being.
- ☐ My life is determined by the traditions of my group without question.
- ☐ My life is determined by my group, but with lots of resistance.
- ☐ My life is determined by myself, but with lots of guilt.
- ☐ My life is determined by myself.
- ☐
- ☐
- ☐

Orthodoxy is the death of intelligence.

—Bertrand Russell

Beliefs about Suffering

- [ ] Life is a drag.
- [ ] Life is joyful.
- [ ] I cause my own suffering.
- [ ] Others (people, places, and things) cause my suffering.
- [ ] Suffering is inescapable.
- [ ] Suffering can be transcended.
- [ ] Suffering is punishment.
- [ ] Suffering is a gift for growth.
- [ ] Suffering is the result of attachments.
- [ ] No pain, no gain.
- [ ] Grin and bear it.
- [ ] That's life! (Sinatra)
- [ ] Only "bad" people suffer.
- [ ] Bad things can happen to good people. (Rabbi Kushner)
- [ ]
- [ ]
- [ ]

Beliefs about Sex

- [ ] Sex is spiritual.
- [ ] Sex is evil and dirty.
- [ ] Sex is a weapon.
- [ ] Sex is a gift and communication.
- [ ] Sex is a mere biological function like itching or sneezing
- [ ] Sex is a necessary evil.
- [ ] Sex is a three-letter word.
- [ ] Sex is frightening.
- [ ] Sex is an invitation.
- [ ] There is a proper and moral sexuality.
- [ ] There are as many sexualities as there are people.
- [ ] Sex is a commodity.
- [ ] Sex is a possession.
- [ ] Sex should be free and easy.
- [ ] Sex is part of a complete human life.
- [ ] Celibacy and abstinence lead to God.
- [ ] Sexual activity is one of God's dances.
- [ ]
- [ ]
- [ ]

Beliefs about Money

☐ Money is the measure of personal worth.
☐ Money is the root of all evil.
☐ I don't like to talk about money.
☐ I do my work for the money.
☐ I do my work because it fulfills me.
☐ I am proud of money.
☐ I am ashamed about money.

☐ Money is a symbol of energy.
☐ Money is power.
☐ Money = freedom.
☐ Money is slavery and oppression.
☐
☐
☐

Beliefs about Power

☐ I have the power to change my life.
☐ I am powerless.
☐ Power is hereditary.
☐ Power can be attained.
☐ Power is corruption.
☐ Power can be used for good.

☐ I am subject to the powers that be.
☐ I have all power within myself.
☐
☐
☐

Beliefs about Emotions

☐ It is a sign of weakness to show emotion.
☐ It is a sign of strength to show emotion.
☐ I repress bad emotions.
☐ I repress good emotions.
☐ I express all emotions.

☐ Emotions are not real.
☐ Emotions are more real than thoughts.
☐
☐
☐

You're nothing but a set of obsolete responses.

—T. S. Eliot

Beliefs about Thoughts

- [ ] My thinking reflects reality.
- [ ] My thinking creates reality.
- [ ] My thinking distorts reality.
- [ ] My thinking is an electrical and biochemical process.
- [ ] My thoughts digest experience.
- [ ] My thoughts are like a computer program.
- [ ] My thoughts are always right.
- [ ] My thoughts are shameful and unworthy.
- [ ] Our brains are too big for their britches.
- [ ] Thinking makes it so.
- [ ] Thinking is a waste of time.
- [ ] Other people don't think like me.
- [ ] Everyone has these thoughts.
- [ ] I think a lot about what others think of me.
- [ ] I feel trapped in my thinking.
- [ ] My thinking frees me.
- [ ] I must not think bad thoughts.
- [ ] I must consider every possibility.
- [ ] Thinking about sin is as good as committing the sin.
- [ ] God can read my thoughts.
- [ ] Others can tell what I'm thinking.
- [ ] Nobody will ever really know what I really think.
- [ ]
- [ ]
- [ ]

Beliefs about Love

- [ ] I am unlovable
- [ ] I am incapable of loving.
- [ ] I am full of love.
- [ ] Love is all you need. (Beatles)
- [ ] Love stinks. (J. Geils)
- [ ] Love is the highest spiritual attainment.
- [ ] Love is a sign of weakness.
- [ ] Love is only for my family or group.
- [ ] Love is the flip side of hate.
- [ ] Love is only in the movies.
- [ ] Unconditional love is possible.
- [ ] Love is not possible.
- [ ] Love means never having to say you're sorry.
- [ ] Love is sappy.
- [ ] Love is slavery.
- [ ] Love is freedom.
- [ ] Love is for others.
- [ ]
- [ ]
- [ ]

Beliefs about Beliefs

- [ ] Beliefs are accurate measures of reality.
- [ ] Beliefs are harmless.
- [ ] Beliefs are hurtful.
- [ ] One cannot live without beliefs.
- [ ] There is only one right way to believe.
- [ ] I believe in beliefs.
- [ ] I believe in myself.
- [ ] I believe beliefs are tools.
- [ ] I believe beliefs are rules.
- [ ] I believe I can change my beliefs.
- [ ] I am stuck with my beliefs; it's too late to change.
- [ ] I stand up for my beliefs.
- [ ] I change my beliefs to suit my peers and situation.
- [ ] A person with beliefs is morally and spiritually bankrupt.
- [ ] A person without beliefs is a secure person.
- [ ] Beliefs are a map.
- [ ] Beliefs are the destination.
- [ ] Believing makes it so.
- [ ] Believing is an art form.
- [ ] Beliefs are limits to be transcended. (John Lilly)
- [ ] Beliefs are our way of interpreting the world in symbols.
- [ ] Beliefs cause suffering.
- [ ] Beliefs can cause freedom.
- [ ] Believe it or not!
- [ ]
- [ ]
- [ ]

> The moment we want to be something we are no longer free.
>
> —Krishnamurti

Beliefs about Authority

- [ ] Authority is always right.
- [ ] Authority is always wrong.
- [ ] Authority is earned.
- [ ] Question authority.
- [ ] Authority is granted by others.
- [ ] Authority is a privilege, not a right.
- [ ] Authority is a divine right and infallible.
- [ ] Authority will take responsibility for my actions.
- [ ] I am responsible for my actions even if so instructed by authority.
- [ ] Authority derives from below.
- [ ] Authority is granted from above.
- [ ]
- [ ]
- [ ]

Beliefs about Status

☐ I care what others think of me.
☐ I don't give a hoot.
☐ I care when appropriate.
☐ I only feel "real" when I stand out from the crowd.
☐ Keep up with the Joneses.
☐ Status means material goods, money, and position.
☐ Status is self-granted and based on values.
☐ I fear ridicule of my peers most of all.
☐ I invite ridicule as confirmation of my "uniqueness."

☐ Current cultural fashions of thought and behavior are important.
☐ There are eternal standards of human value, not just temporal.
☐ I am sensitive to the approval of people I respect.
☐ I am sensitive to the approval of those I don't even know or respect.
☐
☐
☐

Beliefs about Family

☐ Like father, like son.
☐ The apple doesn't fall far from the tree.
☐ If you want to see your spouse in twenty years, look at their parent.
☐ One must never betray the family secrets or skeletons.
☐ Parents are always right.
☐ Children should be seen and not heard.
☐ Families are partnerships.
☐ Families are prisons.
☐ The sins of the parents are visited upon the children.
☐ It is possible to break the generational pattern of families.

☐ One can outgrow the "inner parent" or critic.
☐ Parents are biological.
☐ Parent figures can be found outside the home.
☐ Our behavior patterns and responses are conditioned by early family.
☐ Our behaviors are solely our own decisions.
☐ Genetics determine one's fate.
☐ Genetics can contribute.
☐ Genetics can be transcended and self-transformed to a degree.

- [ ] You hear your voice talking to your children and hear your parent's voice as yours.
- [ ] I would have chosen another family.
- [ ] I like my family.
- [ ] I hate my upbringing but wouldn't trade it nonetheless.
- [ ] The child is father to the "man," mother to the woman.

- [ ] I have to live up to my given name.
- [ ] My given name is irrelevant and doesn't affect who I am.
- [ ]
- [ ]
- [ ]

> Gentleness is dignified, but caution is debasing; only a noble fearlessness can give wings to the mind, with which to soar beyond the common ken.
>
> —Margaret Fuller

Beliefs about Intimacy

- [ ] Honesty is the best policy.
- [ ] You can't trust anyone.
- [ ] You can never ever know another person really.
- [ ] Honesty hurts but is movement toward growth.
- [ ] I find it hard to say "I love you."
- [ ] I say I love you but don't feel it.
- [ ] Physical touch is repulsive.

- [ ] Physicality is wordless communication.
- [ ] If I'm honest and share, I am surrendering power to another.
- [ ] Intimacy is weakness.
- [ ]
- [ ]
- [ ]

Beliefs about Substances

- [ ] Eat to live.
- [ ] Live to eat.
- [ ] You are what you eat.
- [ ] Addictions = no will power.
- [ ] Addictions are a disease.
- [ ] Addictions are caused by rigid beliefs.
- [ ] Anything can become an addiction.
- [ ] Beliefs are addictions.

- [ ] Substances can enhance life.
- [ ] Substances lessen the quality of life.
- [ ] Substances are a substitute for life.
- [ ] Life itself is a substance we are addicted to.
- [ ]
- [ ]
- [ ]

Beliefs about Mortality

- [ ] Death is like sleep.
- [ ] Death is a passage.
- [ ] Death is merely the irrevocable extinction of consciousness.
- [ ] Death is rebirth.
- [ ] He not busy being born is busy dying. (Dylan).
- [ ] When you die, you go to heaven.
- [ ] We are already dead and in hell.
- [ ] We are already dead and in heaven.
- [ ] Heaven and hell, life and death all exist simultaneously and right here and now.
- [ ] I don't like to think about it.
- [ ] Other people die.
- [ ] I always think about it.
- [ ] It's important to leave something behind to make a difference and to be remembered by.
- [ ] Personal "fame" after death doesn't matter.
- [ ] Don't consider death much, accept it as part of a natural process.
- [ ] Would accept immortality if offered.
- [ ] Would refuse.
- [ ] Suicide is an option.
- [ ] Not an option.
- [ ] Doesn't seem real to me somehow.
- [ ] Already dead, so not able to check off these little boxes.
- [ ]
- [ ]
- [ ]

Beliefs about Work

- [ ] All work and no play makes Jill a dull girl.
- [ ] Idle hands are the devil's playground.
- [ ] Play is as important as work.
- [ ] Play is frivolous and nonproductive.
- [ ] Self-image is derived from working.
- [ ] Work is morally correct.
- [ ] Some forms of work are more "important" than others.
- [ ] Play should be equivalent to work.
- [ ] I feel guilty and frivolous when playing.
- [ ] You should work at what you love.
- [ ] Time to get to work on this book.
- [ ]
- [ ]
- [ ]

First SHAVE

Who We're Supposed to Be

Who are we supposed to be?

As soon as we're born,
we're assigned names, religions, ethnicities, and even ideologies
we never chose.
These beliefs about self are
the first stuffings
our skulls receive.
We take these things for granted, assuming these definitions are
who we're supposed to be,
rarely questioning
their validity for our lives.

Who are we supposed to be?

For many of us, it is preordained.
For many of us,
it has the tragic aspects of an accident . . .

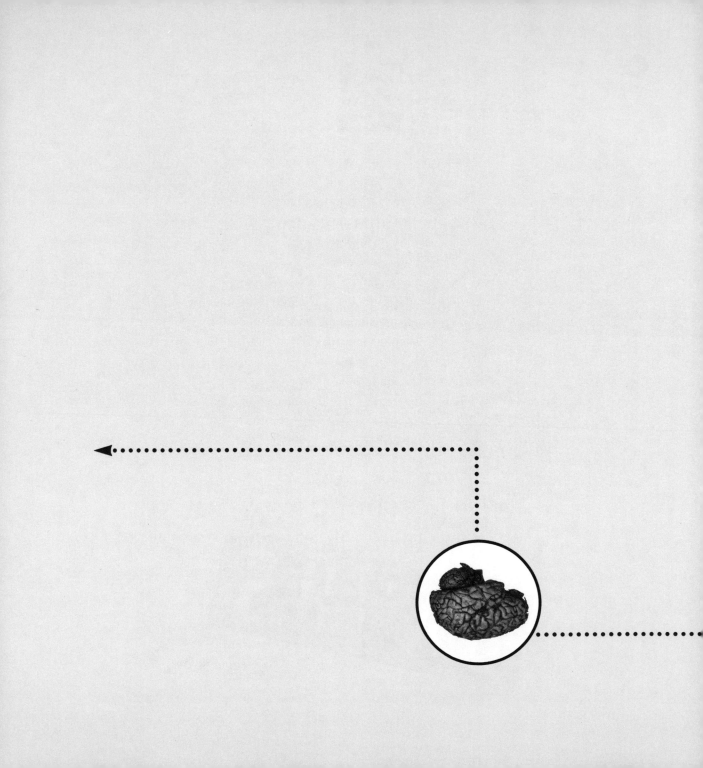

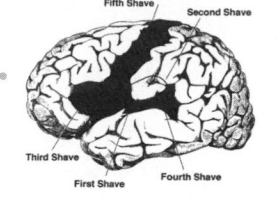

Fifth Shave Second Shave
Third Shave Fourth Shave
First Shave

AT THE SCENE OF THE ACCIDENT

It seems as if we've been involved in an accident and wake up at the scene finding we're the only survivors. Our births and lives surely seem this way. We don't remember asking to be born or to become involved in any way, yet here we are, innocent bystanders and guilty parties alike, numb and in shock, at the scene of the accident, weaving and wandering our way through the wreckage and traffic of our lives, foggily trying to remember the details and get out of further harm's way. We seem to have suffered brain damage as a result, having no memory of how we got here and even less about where we're going.

We live the rest of our lives in shock, by accident, accepting the "tragic" circumstances of our fate; knuckling under to the directions of everybody and everything else around the scene of "our" accident, pretending to be officials and in the know. While we may seem to make choices and "be ourselves," we are really just treating our life as an accident and either bemoaning our ill fortune in resignation or idly shrugging it off and settling for what the insurance company of peers and authorities have to offer. It could be worse, right? they tell us assuredly. We begin to believe it ourselves, settling for less.

> Every man's foremost task is the actualization of his unique, unprecedented, and never-recurring potentialities, and not the repetition of something that another has already achieved.
>
> —Martin Buber

Accidental Lives?

Still numb and adrift from happenstance to circumstance, never becoming fully healed and alive, never setting out to see what would happen if we didn't live our lives by accident. This IS your life and at its end, you can't say, as you would of spilt milk, "Sorry, it was just an accident." But then again, maybe you can. It's up to each of us.

You must become who you are. A life lived willy-nilly and at the whims of fashionable beliefs is a life not really lived at all, but a role inhabited by a stranger. It is a life on route to a head-on collision with regret, rage, and deception. By treating your life as an accident and therefore worthless and to be lived unmindfully, you deceive yourself most profoundly. Only when you understand this will you experience rage and regret at the forces within you and outside of you that have kept your potential and true self locked away like a dirty secret you had no right to know.

It is not only your right, it is also your obligation to reclaim your true self from the scene of the accident and to inhabit it fully, no matter the cost or outcry. All the survivors of this accident have the same potential to recover from the trauma of discovering that we're alive and that it's not going to last. All of us have the resources to wake up from the anesthesia of our "beliefs" and fears and to claim the health and growth that we paid for in full through our births and eventual deaths. We had no choice in terms of payment and collection. We do have a choice in how we will spend what is left.

Our True Selves

A well-known axiom exhorts us: "To thine own self be true." It rolls glibly off tongues, is engraved on medallions, and is touted as a universal truth. However, every time we've ever attempted to be true to ourselves, we're pulled back into the fold of the accident-prone and made to feel like traitors, weirdos, or worse. We're told to let others ask and answer the fundamental questions of our lives. Somehow, perhaps by accident, we gradually assent, knuckle under, and forget our great promise and confuse our true self with the slogan.

Who are these people and forces that act like such a powerful undertow, dragging us into the murky depths of sleep and slavery? Most of the time, it is we, ourselves, out of fear, habit, and conditioning. We make willing victims of ourselves and continue to protest as we drag ourselves away into golden cages.

What we want is to become ourselves. Nothing that is should be suppressed; nothing is superfluous.
—Friedrich Nietzsche

I must create a System or be enslav'd by another man's.
—William Blake

A Deliberate Life

To examine our lives and make them worth living is the first step toward acting deliberately and not accidentally. Said Thoreau about his stay at Walden, "I went to the woods because I wished to live deliberately, to front only the essential facts of life, and see if I could not learn what it had to teach, and not, when I came to die, discover that I had not lived."

The word "deliberately" stems from the word "deliberation," and what it means is that we must *think*. If we think that our lives are accidents, then accidents they will surely be. It's probably a miracle and only an accident itself that we escaped to even begin to think about things such as this.

Sometimes it seems as if we live out our lives in the attic of the house of our being, rarely visiting the first and second floors and never the basement, which is locked.

—Jean Houston

Belief Systems

Any belief system seeks to answer these qualms by imposing its own structure over your unique questions, appealing subtly and insidiously to your deepest fears and longings. It wraps itself obligingly around your psyche and synapses, becoming a parasite and not the symbiotic partner you expected. It is almost a case of demonic possession.

Beliefs and expectations all contain very important truths, questions, and occasional answers, yet at a very profound level they are not *your* truths, questions, or answers. By accepting the free bread they offer, we only mask the real hunger we have for true fulfillment. This hunger can be appeased only by our own efforts, by the planting and raising of our own questions, by harvesting our own answers, and by baking our own truths. Only then will we deserve to live deliberately, mindfully, and call ourselves truly alive.

We will be able to resist the temptingly easy junk-food handouts offered us by systems of belief and thought which keep us on the spiritual dole and render us incapable of fending for ourselves, incapable of becoming who we really are. If we, in our hunger, agree to feed from the plate of fear and guilt that we serve ourselves, we foster the accidental life.

Don't compromise yourself. You are all you've got.

—Janis Joplin

Most systems of belief are merely the decayed and fossilized remains of what one person did in deliberation and mindfulness for themselves.

Will we be content to live on the dry crumbs of their long-dead labors? Or will we take them at their word; that what they accomplished is likewise possible for us as well; that we, too, can take charge of our lives and reach deeply enough to pull out what gives us joy and meaning.

An Examined Life

A life lived unexamined is a second-hand life. It is second-hand because it is dependent upon things other than itself for meaning. Take these away and you take away the meaning. An examined life is meaningful because the examination itself grants meaning and dignity. Surely that is all the meaning we have need of. A life lived deliberately draws meaning from itself and derives both dignity and fulfillment from its quest. To reclaim one's true self, rather than leaving it spilt at the scene of the accident, is to reclaim our personal right to deliberation.

Do we want off-the-shelf answers and one-size-fits-all truths or are we going to make our own? The choice has always been ours. The fact that we even have this choice is a secret that's been kept from us nearly forever by ourselves and by the systems with which we crucify ourselves.

To become who we really are, we must live our lives on purpose, deliberately, as though we really meant it—not accidentally. The road of life is safer and wider than we've been led to believe.

Don't worry; please, please. How many times do I have to say it? There's no way not to be who you are and where.

—Zen Master Ikkyu

We live only part of the life we are given.

—Michael Murphy

Who we're **supposed** to be becomes "normal" after a while. The beliefs about self we acquired by accident are constantly reinforced by our families, friends, culture, and media. For many of us, our biggest fear is rejection, of not appearing "normal." Through our fear, we worsen the

accident and become steadily more
alienated from our truest selves,
conforming to the most accepted and
lowest possible common denominator.

Who are we supposed to be?

Well . . . , "normal."

Whatever your age, your upbringing, or your education, what you are made of is mostly unused potential.

—George Leonard

Only by living absurdly can we change this absurd life.

—Ecuadoran graffiti (translated by Michael Gill)

So strong is the belief in life,
in what is most fragile in
life—real life, I mean—that
in the end this belief is lost.

—André Breton

The ways of
constructively
transforming the mind
are to cause mistaken states
of consciousness not to be
generated and good states
of consciousness to be both
generated and increased.

—His Holiness
the Dalai Lama

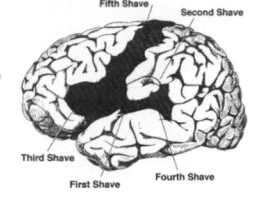

DEFINE NORMYL

I was very young when I began to think seriously about beliefs. I had just recently fled from a family where I was being emotionally and physically forced into a shape they thought would fit their beliefs about their son, themselves, and their world. They wanted me to be who I was *supposed to be:* normal.

When I tried to be just myself, I was rejected.

I was held captive by an educational system that sought to compulsorily condition me with its beliefs about what knowledge I should have access to and what my role in society's machinery would be. The goal was normal kids.

When I actually tried to learn, I was either failed or ignored.

I was trying desperately to escape the insidious traps set for me by the religion of my childhood, which had ruthlessly sought to twist my young spirit with beliefs that led to shame, guilt, and unworthiness. This was considered normal.

When I didn't measure up, I was condemned to hell.

The government under which all this took place was busy murdering boys not much older than me because of its economic and political beliefs about an Asian country. The government had very definite beliefs about its use for my body when I would turn eighteen. What could be more normal than that?

If I went along with these beliefs, I would probably die in a far-away jungle or be forced to kill another boy. If I didn't go along with these beliefs, I would go to prison.

The commodity-culture economy I was immersed in held out shiny, expensive products as something equivalent to personal worthiness. Everyone, it seemed, wanted these things.

If I worked myself to death struggling to gain these material signs of worth, I was sure I would lose myself. If I didn't accumulate these things, I would be forever seen as a misfit, impoverished and somehow disreputable.

My "peer" group, already brainwashed and conditioned by the beliefs above, became the unwitting agents of their oppressors. Only normal kids fit in, got along, and were team players.

When I tried to be accepted for myself, I was ostracized, made to feel inferior, and ignored.

My self-image couldn't have been lower. Unaware that I was little more than a robot, programmed and manipulated by lethal belief systems, I blamed only myself. How could I ever hope to be normal? I believed myself fatally flawed and doomed to unhappiness, completely unaware that I wasn't the only person in the world to feel this way, that the conspiracy of silence blanketed everyone with a fragile and angry veneer of "normality."

When I tried to transcend these beliefs or examine them more closely, I felt piercing pain, shame, and self-loathing. I came to believe it was useless and that acquiescence or oblivion were the only remedies.

The beliefs of parents, school, church, government, and peers formed a seamless conspiracy. It was becoming clear to me then, and clearer to me now, that my suffering had been caused by beliefs and their true believers. I abandoned any faith in beliefs and became its unwillingly recruited enemy.

For me, this became normal behavior.

Today, I'm writing about nearly the same subject. All that has really changed is my age. Everything else, sadly and predictably enough, remains normally the same.

If you're reading this book, it's safe to assume that you, too, had similar experiences, that you, as well, have some questions about what really constitutes normal behavior.

She lacks confidence, she craves admiration insatiably. She lives on the reflections of herself in the eyes of others. She does not dare to be herself.

—Anaïs Nin

You Don't Get Me Twice

There's a caricature by artist Fons van Woerkom of John Lennon removing a ball and chain from his head. The caption reads, "You don't get me twice." It is obviously the ball and chain of beliefs and conditioning that he is removing. On second glance, he looks like a terrorist about to hurl an old-fashioned bomb at us.

Which one is it? Does it make any difference? I don't think so. The quote from Emerson, in the front of this book, says that the virtue most in demand in society is conformity. Lennon obviously was not conforming by removing the ball and chain from his head. He wasn't being normal.

So long as we conform to the belief systems that enslave our heads and spirits, everything seems fine and we are rewarded, much as rats are for running a maze. Remove that ball and chain, however, and we are suddenly singled out.

Instead of being congratulated for thinking for ourselves, attaining freedom, and becoming real human beings, we are viewed as terrorists and as a menace to the precarious systems built on the quicksands of belief.

It is not half so dangerous to a man to be immured in a dungeon with his God and his own clear conscience as to walk the streets fearing the scrutiny of a thousand eyes.

—Margaret Fuller

Belief as Denial

Jacob Needleman has said that belief is the effort to deny the confusion that is really our normal state. Faith, he says, is a state of being produced by a moment of self-knowledge, a total apprehension of our existential confusion. In other words, faith is acceptance and reality.

In this light, belief is denial and lies. It would appear that one of the only ways to transcend limiting, "normal" belief is to deny harmful belief itself. For many of us, this process entails what is "normally" called a "breakdown."

R. D. Laing has put forth the proposition that psychological breakdowns are actually breakthroughs to enlightenment. The section "Do It Yourself Brain Surgery" (p. 113) takes up these issues in greater detail, arguing that it is only in transcending our conditioning, imprinting, and beliefs that we attain our true selves, a spiritual alchemy wrought in most cases by the fires of suffering; the fire being the tension between what we've been taught to believe and what we truly feel.

If I try to be like him, who will be like me?

—Yiddish proverb

The Imperialization of Consciousness

Many of us begin to suspect that nearly everything around us represents what Theodore Roszak has called "an imperialization of consciousness," a colonization, if you will, of the formerly autonomous territory inside our skulls. Breakdowns and breakthroughs become our means to declare independence from the colonists represented by limiting beliefs and their natural allies, fears.

What the world considers to be "normal" becomes revealed to be an irreconcilable state of inner civil war. We have to discover what is normal for us in order to finally become who we really are, revolting against the belief colonists in our heads and quenching the fires in our souls. We are codes we must crack, riddles we must answer. The answers to what is normal for us are already in our grasp and cannot be found elsewhere.

Normality as Widespread Psychosis

Native American activist and musician John Trudell, on his "Graffiti Man" CD, says that there is "a psychotic pall so widespread as to be assumed normal." When a belief system becomes pervasive and widely unquestioned, it becomes the operating system for the culture and by extension the individual.

Thomas Paine says that "a long habit of not thinking a thing *wrong*, gives it a superficial appearance of being *right*, and raises at first a formidable outcry in defence of custom. But the tumult soon subsides. Time makes more converts than reason." Questioning the system, even a psychotic or normally and rightly appearing *wrong* one, is considered abnormal, and yes, perhaps even psychotic.

This obviously happened in Soviet Russia, where dissenters were confined to mental hospitals. Obviously one must be "insane" to even question what is so obviously the normal way of doing business. In our own and other countries, the incarceration is not often as extreme, but sanctions are applied nonetheless to the one who dares to call the prevailing belief system into question. Nazi Germany is of course the classic and extreme example of a psychotic belief system so "widespread as to be assumed normal."

The burning of witches at Salem, the modern-day witch hunts of McCarthyism, the tragedies of Jonestown and Waco all stand as macabre tributes to the tenacity of smaller enclosed belief systems that became suicidally and homicidally "normal." In

What will become of the creator if I become normal?

—Anaïs Nin

many ways, we ourselves form belief cults of "one" and begin to resemble these larger entities. The burning pyre and Inquisitor's torture rack have been replaced by behavior-control drugs in most cases, but the sentiment remains the same.

Conspiracy and Complacency

Our cooperation in the psychosis of "normality" is insured through fear. In the old days it was fear of banishment into the wilderness or torture. These days it's primarily fear of "not fitting in," "standing out from the crowd," and economic exile that keep us in line and part of the herd on its way to the slaughterhouse of mundane and drab existence.

The least among us is as guilty of complicity as the greatest. The epigram to this book refers to a conspiracy of society. It is a conspiracy that is self-created and self-perpetuating. The relentless influence of media and peer pressure maintains the semblance of "normality" and the conspiracy of silence; what Kenneth Rexroth calls "the Social Lie" and Guy Debord describes as the "Society of the Spectacle."

Elvis Costello in his song "Radio, Radio" blames our compliance on indifference in the promises of security, telling us that the media doesn't give us any choices, that it tells us to listen to reason and do as we're told, because otherwise ". . . they think that it's treason." In this case, treasonous thinking equals questioning the "Spectacle" presented us in the media as the only choice.

We have come to accept street violence as "normal," wars for peace as "normal," and sadly enough, our own self-loathing, gnawing fears, and lack of community and fulfillment as "normal" and as the neurotic price we pay for "modern" life. In fact, violence, war, and even our own feelings of inadequacy have become our entertainment, reducing us to the role of powerless spectators.

Small sacrifices, we "believe," in exchange for a fistful of dollars, status, peer acceptance, and tenuous security. Do we really need to seek the approval of forces we don't respect? Do we really need to keep up with the Jim Joneses?

Are we fulfilled in our roles as mere spectators of "normality" and consumers of normal beliefs? Or are we so alienated from our truest selves that

> The dreamer whose dreams are non-utilitarian has no place in this world. In this world the poet is anathema, the thinker a fool, the artist an escapist, the man of vision a criminal.
>
> —Henry Miller

> You pretend to be more eccentric than you actually are because you worry you are an interchangeable cog.
>
> —Douglas Coupland

we have indeed *become* our accidental fears and now conspire against our own awakening?

Alienation as Normal Behavior

R. D. Laing pioneered a revolutionary concept of what actually constitutes "normal" and "abnormal" during his career of working with schizophrenia. In his influential and essential book, *The Politics of Experience,* he says,

> There are forms of alienation that are relatively strange to statistically "normal" forms of alienation. The "normally" alienated person, by reason of the fact that he acts more or less like everyone else, is taken to be sane. Other forms of alienation that are out of step with the prevailing state of alienation are those that are labeled by the "normal" majority as bad or mad.
>
> The condition of alienation, of being asleep, of being unconscious, of being out of one's mind, is the condition of the normal man.
>
> Society highly values its normal man. It educates children to lose themselves and to become absurd, and thus to be normal.
>
> Normal men have killed perhaps 100,000,000 of their fellow normal men in the last fifty years.
>
> Our behavior is a function of our experience. We act according to the way we see things.
>
> *If our experience is destroyed, our behavior will be destructive.*
>
> If our experience is destroyed, we have lost our own selves.

Stupidity is replicating itself at an astonishing rate. The person who stands up and says, "This is stupid," either is asked to 'behave' or, worse, is greeted with a cheerful, "Yes, we know! Isn't it terrific!"

—Frank Zappa

In other words, if the so-called "normal" way of doing things is insane or "abnormal," then the only sane response will be what most people would consider "insane" behavior. In Krishnamurti's words to the same effect, "It's no measure of health to be well adjusted to a profoundly sick society."

How many times have we been told to "fit in," not to "rock the boat," to be a good "team player," to "go along to get along," to be "who we're supposed to be"? These messages are so pervasive and subtle that we have grown used to them, not even hearing their hypnotic whisper as they reinforce our compliance in what is an insane situation. Only by becoming insane ourselves, can we even begin to consider it and ourselves "normal."

Questioning Normal Beliefs

When we begin to ask questions about all this, we soon find out that there are only a narrowly prescribed set of questions to ask. If we dare to ask really important and penetrating questions, we are silenced with peer pressure, ridicule, or force. We are encouraged to accept the current descriptions of reality as reality itself and to find our meaning reflected in that distorted and consensual mirror.

Many aid in the conspiracy of silence by drowning questions and questing in a sea of alcohol, a fog of drugs, an obsession with the spectacle of sports or television, or any number of socially approved methods. While some of these compulsions are officially frowned upon, they are nonetheless widely accepted and tolerated, even encouraged. At least the person is now acting in a "normal" and understandable fashion. Now they can be dealt with.

Most counseling—either spiritual or psychological therapies—seems to consist of helping one to "cope," to "adjust," and to "fit in" with the current belief systems. In other words, one is subjected to a process of psychological cabinetry, planing a bit off here, a bit of gluing there in order to return the person to service as a properly functioning drawer in the furniture of society.

In the drawer, of course, are neatly folded fashionable beliefs and crisp and correct opinions. This is called being a "productive member of society." There are no more protesting squeaks as the drawer is used, no more rough spots that resist compliant pushing and pulling.

As Laing says, our own experience is destroyed and we are supplied instead with two-dimensional substitutes. Most people experience this as a sort of unfocused bittersweet regret, usually at late middle age. Others experience it as a nihilistic falling into compulsive disease.

> A person can't be creative and conformist at the same time.
>
> —J. A. Meyer

Resistance to Questioning

So you can see that most of our attempts to "become ourselves" or to "find ourselves" are doomed to either failure or, at the very least, resistance on the part of those around us, who consider our efforts to become real human beings "abnormal."

Young people are given a couple of years leeway in this enterprise. "Oh, she's still 'finding herself.' She'll 'settle down' in a couple of years," says the mother, knowingly. "He's just busy 'sowing his wild oats,'" says the father proudly. Wild oats sown and self found, the children settle down. Their adolescent rebellion and behavior is seen as "normal" only if it eventually knuckles under and they become *who they're supposed to be.*

If the youth attains true sanity and continues to question the widely accepted belief systems of the culture, then he or she is obviously "sick" and in need of some adjustment, maybe a stint in the armed services to become a "man" or a marriage and baby to become a "woman." This is "normal."

Taken Hostage

Another model for our situation is found in the psychology of hostage situations. We rationalize these "isolated" acts as being committed by solitary, fanatic, or crazed ("abnormal") personalities, far indeed from where we sit in "civilized" ("normal") society, secretly grateful that it isn't we who are held hostage; thankful that no ransom is being demanded for our lives.

We are so far gone in our own hostage situation that we no longer recognize that we ourselves are hostages on a much grander and subtler level and that ransom is being demanded every moment in the form of fear, dread, and unfulfillment for our membership among the "normal" hostages.

Psychologists have long identified a behavior peculiar to those who have been held hostage called the "Stockton syndrome." Basically, the model developed says that people taken hostage sooner or later sympathize and even identify with their captors.

The most famous and extreme example in recent times of the Stockton Syndrome is that of Patty Hearst and the Symbionese Liberation Army. Kidnapped against her will, she eventually joined the group in its activities, even to the point of being

Normality is what cuts off your sixth finger and your tail.
—member of the Church of the Sub-Genius

videotaped as she aided in a bank robbery, holding a weapon. Other less extreme cases involve the released hostage justifying their captor's causes and eventually lobbying on their behalf.

Of course, it is obvious at once that taking on the beliefs of one's armed and dangerous captors is pretty good insurance for survival. Struggle and argument in such a situation could only prove painful, at best. And so the process proceeds. In one way or another, we take on the beliefs of our captors as a survival technique and become their aiders and abettors.

Belief as Weapons

Tribal, regional, and national belief systems capture their hostages with cunningly crafted psychological and spiritual weapons disguised as beliefs that appeal to our programming for sleep, easy answers, father figures, abdication of personal responsibility, rage, and the urge to place the blame elsewhere. What threat and danger do we find in these weapons of belief that so easily make us hostages? Fear of being different, fear of being left out, fear of economic reprisal and, most of all, fear of not appearing "normal."

On a less obviously vicious level, the syndrome is at work in more or less mainstream political organizations, religions, economic, educational, and social institutions. Every organization, no matter its size, can be identified in some way as a cult or hostage situation, in its structure, appeal, recruitment, and indoctrination. When the hostage situation becomes big and widespread enough, like a church, government, or corporation, it becomes the powerful norm and is entitled to label others as terrorists, heretics, or traitors; in short: abnormal. Abnormality has, as usual, become normal.

Voices in Our Heads

In his book *The Sirens of Titan,* Kurt Vonnegut creates a military culture on Mars that is controlled by the surgical implantation of an antenna in people's skulls. If they so much as think unsanctioned or "abnormal" thoughts, or question the prevailing belief system, they receive painful shocks in their brains. They are, of course, easily controlled, and what passes for normality is never questioned.

While we may not *yet* have real wires buried in our scalps, perhaps they

> To set out to *just* be different for its own sake is to actually surrender to the easiest path of all, which is to be superficial . . . You should feel completely normal within yourself.
>
> —Genesis P-Orridge

are becoming unnecessary, anyway. Easy acceptance of slogans and a nearly visceral fear of the disapproval of our peers is the stick that keeps us in line and who we're supposed to be.

Vonnegut describes the process of awakening from the "normality" of the pain-giving wire in the head and (for these people) nearly literally shaving the inside of your skull:

Unk, old friend, almost everything I know for sure has come from fighting the pain from my antenna, *said the letter to Unk*. Whenever I start to turn my head and look at something, and the pain comes, I keep turning my head anyway, because I know I am going to see something I'm not supposed to see. Whenever I ask a question, and the pain comes, I know I have asked a really good question. Then I break the question into little pieces, and I ask the pieces of the questions. Then I get answers to the pieces, and then I put the answers all together and get an answer to the big question.

The more pain I train myself to stand, the more I learn. You are afraid of the pain now, Unk, but you won't learn anything if you don't invite the pain. And the more you learn, the gladder you will be to stand the pain.

Courage and Cowardice

Unitarian minister and abolitionist Theodore Parker mentions in his memoirs that one of his earliest spiritual influences was that of being held up by his mother to read the monument in Lexington, Massachusetts, dedicated to the Revolutionary War Minutemen. On the monument was carved:

"REBELLION TO TYRANTS IS OBEDIENCE TO GOD."

We have to look within as well as without for the forms of tyranny that seek our slavery and, like Parker, become our own abolitionists, daring to defy the "normality" of our own slavery. Doing this, we obey the universal law. Rebelling against limiting beliefs, we become fully human and awake.

"Consciousness has made cowards of us all," says social critic Camille Paglia.

Esalen's Law:
1) You always teach others what you most need to learn yourself.
2) You are your own worst student.
—Richard Price

The precious gift of awareness is shoehorned into shapes all sickeningly alike and normal. Pain, intellectual or spiritual, is avoided and discouraged at all costs.

It takes real courage to try to wake up, to become *who you really are*. True consciousness requires heroism, not cowardice. Only by standing out do we actually begin to fit in. Only by shaking things up do they finally fall into place. Only by acting "abnormally" do we even begin to feel what is "normal" for us.

To become yourself is actually the most normal thing there is, no matter what you will surely be told by the subtle antenna in your head or the widespread psychosis around you. Anything else is just crazy. *Abnormal,* really.

Define normyl? Try "hostage." Try "insane." Try "asleep." Try "coward." Try "silent." Try "addicted." Try "alienated." Just try . . .

In the world to come I shall not be asked: "Why were you not Moses?" I shall be asked: "Why were you not Susya?"

—Rabbi Susya

To be original, or different,
is felt to be "dangerous."

—Carl Rogers

First Set of RAZORS

Who we're supposed to be
is determined by the accidental way
in which we acquire beliefs about who we are
and what is considered "normal."

Who we really are
can be examined through razors,
which examine some basic, usually unquestioned assumptions
about ourselves such as
our names, births, families, and genders.
Do we have any choice in these things?

What is "normal" for us?
Use these first razors to find out.

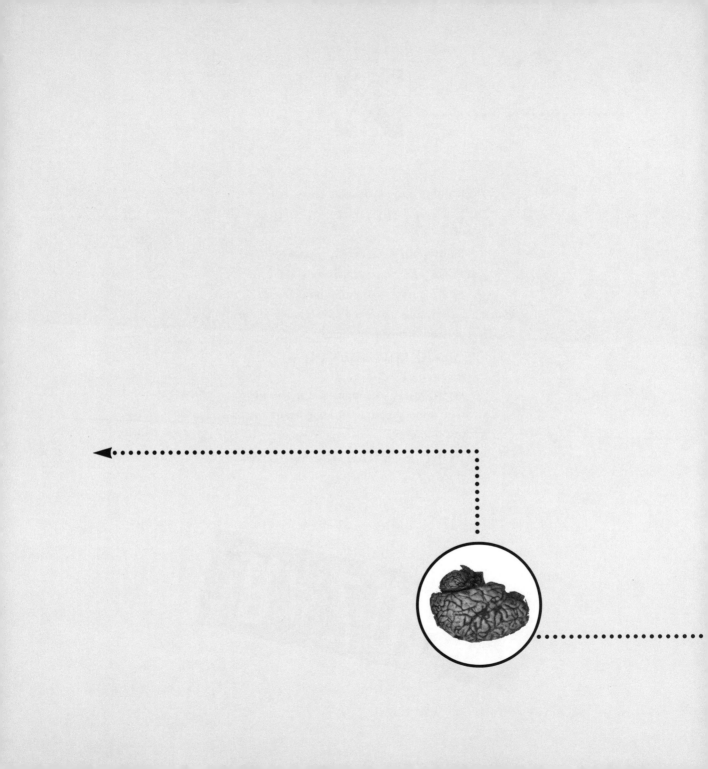

Define Normyl

Just try! Study the chart that follows. It represents a continuum of "normal" beliefs starting at zero. Ascending numbers represent a loosening of rigid beliefs about normality and possibility.
Descending numbers indicate a solidifying of belief and ever more
narrow definitions of what is accepted as normal

Start off by studying the types of beliefs and the examples
I've provided, which are completely arbitrary. You are free to agree or disagree by supplying your own examples in the empty boxes. Be sure to place your own name on the
chart in as honest a position as you are able.

When you've finished with this book, refer back to this activity. Would you now
have different examples? Has your own location of normality shifted? Fill out the chart
with family or a group of friends as well. A lively discussion of what constitutes "normal" is guaranteed to ensue!

Are You Descended from Space Aliens?

This is the recurrent supermarket tabloid headline. The answer is yes, of course you are. You've always suspected this, I'm sure. It explains a lot: like why you're the only "normal" one on this planet and why you always feel so isolated, lonely, and weird. If you accept your extraterrestrial ancestry or not, act as though you do for an hour, a day, or a week.

Your razor: You've been sent here as a galactic anthropologist on a seventy-year mission to study the dominant "intelligent" life form on the planet. You just now remembered this genetically encoded mission in the midst of your cleverly disguised life as a human being.

You must study the humans' beliefs, habits, and behaviors uncritically, coldly even, as an outsider, attempting to determine if they should be allowed entry into the Galactic Federation or simply exterminated as a threat to cosmic well-being.

Detach yourself emotionally from the species and their drama. Examine them as you would a hill of ants or hive of bees. Draw your own conclusions when the mission is completed. Please list three beliefs of the earthlings that you find completely alien and that they themselves consider "normal."

Who Am "I"?

Speak without the use of possessives or personal pronouns, such as I, me, mine. First, a story:

An Hasidic rebbe heard someone calling outside his home. "Who is it?" he called.

"It is I!" replied the voice, recognized as one of his students. The rebbe refused to answer or let the student in until he said his name, explaining that there is only one "I," God, meaning that when we are full of our small "I"s, there is no room for anything greater.

Using the pronoun "I" or its possessive forms, we claim false divinity and solidify our beliefs about the immutability of our conditional personalities. Everything becomes egocentric and we expect the world to revolve solely around our selves. It, of course, does not, and we suffer.

		My Image	Your Image
Abnormal 4	Beliefs Transcended	*Buddha, Gandhi, Krishnamurti, Baal-Shem Tov*	
Abnormal 3	Unconventional Beliefs Generated	*John Lennon, Nietzsche, Thomas Merton, Emerson, Einstein, Timothy Leary, Surrealists*	
Abnormal 2	Conventional Beliefs Questioned	*Thomas Paine, Alan Watts, Bob Dylan, Punk Rock, Beats, Your Author*	
Abnormal 1	Conventional Beliefs in Flux	*Students in General, Trauma as a Condition of . . . , 12 Step Programs, Optimism*	
Normal 0	Conventional Accepted Beliefs	*Ward & June Cleaver, Ozzie & Harriet, Reliance on Clichés, "The Almighty Dollar," Anything Outside is "Abnormal"*	
Abnormal 1	Conventional Beliefs Unquestioned	*Most Spiritual & Secular Leaders, Consumerism, Cynicism Disguised as Acceptance*	
Abnormal 2	Conventional Beliefs Compulsively Defended	*Radio Call-Ins, Addicts, Creation of Religions, Nixon, Pessimism*	
Abnormal 3	Conventional Beliefs Forced on Others	*Religious Fundamentalism, Political Interventions, Social Ostracism, Racism*	
Abnormal 4	Beliefs Transcend Individual	*Hitler, Jim Jones, Cults, Stalinism, Inquisition, Nihilism*	

Try speaking for a while without referring to yourself. It's a lot harder than it sounds. Try this with a sympathetic friend for five minutes. Every time you use a possessive or refer to "I," "me," or "mine," note it. How many times did you return to your "accidental" I? Was it on purpose, or as I suspect, an accident, just force of habit?

Try this when you're alone as well, examining your thoughts as you think them, making the effort to drop the personal reference.

Where are You? Part 1

An Hasidic story told by Rabbi Hanokh: There was a very stupid man who, when he got up each morning, couldn't find his clothes. It got so bad he considered not sleeping. One night, as he undressed, he wrote down exactly where he put everything as he took it off. The next morning, he took the piece of paper and read "cap." There it was and he put it on his head. Then "pants." There they were and he put them on. He continued this until he was completely dressed. "Wonderful," he said, but, adding with great bewilderment, "Where in the world am I?" He looked everywhere, but couldn't find himself. Said Rabbi Hanokh, "This is how it is with us."

This book is like the list the stupid man made of his clothes. So, too, every belief system. How is it with you?

Put a note above your mirror in the bathroom saying, "Here I am" or use lipstick or marker on the mirror itself. A very simple solution to the age-old quest called "finding yourself."

Where Are You? Part 2

This is adapted from an Hasidic parable. Go out into the mountains or empty, canyonlike city streets and make demands by yelling to God (or your true, deliberate self): "Where are you? Show yourself!"

Listen carefully and you'll hear an answer, an echo returning, saying, "Where are you? Show yourself!" Really do this one, no matter how foolish you might feel. It is our feelings of appearing foolish or abnormal that prevent this dialogue from ever happening in the first place. No question, no answers.

Where Do You Live?

Do you know where you live? Quite often, our domicile is as accidental as our identities. It has become "normal" for us to be unaware of formerly vital information.

Poet Gary Snyder says that most people are completely ignorant of their bio-regions. What does he mean by this?

A razor for you: What is the name of your local watershed? Where does your water come from? Can you name two plants that are indigenous only to your area? Animals and insects too? What was the native name for your region?

Better yet, what was the name of the native people who lived/live here? All politics are local, said the late Tip O'Neill. All ecology, too! Our beliefs about things as simple and essential as where we live are usually, shall I say, groundless? Our accidental and normal selves are determined in part by location. Locate yourself.

The Game of Life

Get hold of a spin dial from an old kid's game or make one. Divide it into quadrants. Divide these quadrants into three sections each. In the first quadrant, write: White, Black, Asian, or any three races.

In the next, write poor, rich, middle class. In the third, drop-out, high school, doctorate (or male, female, gay). In the last: slum, suburbia, rural, (Mars?). Any similar descriptions will do.

Spin the dial in this game of life until you get a description for each quadrant. Write down the descriptions after your name, as in: "I am a poor, gay, rural White person.

Imagine the sort of life you might now be leading after the four spins. Reflect on what different beliefs might be formed by those conditions chosen for you at chance, accidentally, on the dial.

Better yet, use four dice or small square cardboard boxes, writing similar descriptions on each side (this will give you six descriptions of gender, class, education, and so forth.) What we thought to be true turns out to be just a genetic and economic crapshoot, after all.

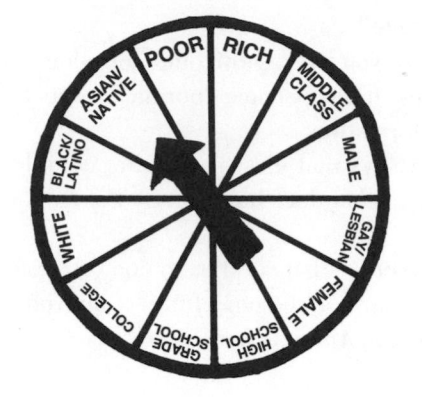

Your Other Lives

If you couldn't have lived this life, which life would you have consciously chosen, unlike the crapshoot of the previous razor? I know you think about this already when people think you're asleep.

Write a short autobiography of three or four paragraphs looking back on this other life in a notebook, including historical period, personal details, etc. Include made-up photos and documents from magazines and yard sales, if you like.

Show it to people and brag about what a great life it was. Maybe they'll be inspired to share their secret lives with you as well. In this way, we can get to really know each other, fantasies and fears included.

Re-create and write yourself daily. You are a character in your own living book. You have a choice in this. You can alter the script. Your "other life" is a good practice. Be thinking about the musical score as well.

Paper Doll Lives

Cut out your face from a photo. Place it on other bodies in magazines, newspapers, etc. See "yourself" in different settings, atop different bodies, yourself as a paper doll.

Shaking hands with Nixon! Singing "Heartbreak Hotel"! Being led to the guillotine. Begging on the street. Making love to movie stars. Preaching sermons. Serving time. Hundreds of alternative realities are yours for the snipping. Yes, these could be your lives. This exercise will make you think about your reactions and feelings in totally different environments and question the permanency of your beliefs as contingent upon history, birth, and circumstance.

Old People's Lives

Spend time with an older person. Ask them to tell you their life story. Put aside enough time for this, perhaps an afternoon. Listen to them. I mean *really* listen. Many of my best friends are over seventy years old.

While they tell you their life story, shut up and listen. Shut off your inner dialogue and questioning. You might learn something. You might have some of your beliefs challenged. You might find out, as I have, that older often equals younger as well as wiser. "I was so much older then," they often tell me, as did Bob Dylan, "but I'm younger than that now."

Your razor: This week, shut off that TV or stereo or computer. Close this book. Skip the mall. Believe someone else's beliefs for a time and live their life. Look for clues as to what they consider "normal."

Ask about "accidental" beliefs in their lives. If there are no "old" people in your life, call a nursing home and adopt an older, lonely friend.

How Old Are You Really?

My grandmother, after looking in the mirror at her sixty-six-year-old face, always looked shocked, saying she was really still a sixteen-year-old girl in Iowa. How does an age-determined point of view affect your beliefs and worldview, your ideas about who you're supposed to be?

I'm around sixteen and a half myself.

It's not how old you are, but how you are old.

—Marie Dressler

The razor: How old is the "you" that you think you are? Ask others.

Show Me Your Face!

The perennial Zen question asked of beginning students is: What was your face before you were born?

The question is a Zen koan, or paradoxical question, designed to force an expansion of consciousness and intuitive leap in the student. There is no way you can rationally answer this or any other koan other than to plant the question in your mind like a seed, watering it with your occasional reflection.

> No place can be found in which to put the Original Face;
> It will not disappear even when the universe is destroyed.
>
> —Mumon

For starters, sit quietly and mentally repeat the question, "What was my original face before I was born?" over and over for about ten minutes. Return to the question in the morning as you awaken and repeat it before you go to sleep.

Eventually some sort of personal insight will dawn upon you, perhaps in the unlikeliest of places and times. Along with the insight will also come a flash of recognition. You've known your original face all along. It is the face you wore before you embarked upon the "accidental" life and assumed the "normal" masks provided you.

Show Me Your Mask!

Make a mask using a paper plate or bag. On it, draw or paint your original face, the face that Zen teaches was your face before your parents had you. If you haven't yet remembered your original face, then make one up. Or paint your true self's face, the one you see reflected in the sad mirror of your heart when alone.

Is it sad? Is it happy? Is it angry, betrayed, transcendent, or elated? Make these masks regularly and hang them around to remind you of your self-examination. Have everybody do it as a party activity, providing plenty of materials. People can then attempt to guess what the masks represent.

We wear masks all the time, different ones for home, work, and solitude. Shaving the inside of your skull is also about ridding ourselves of masks. By making exterior masks, we can start to expose our interior true faces.

Our faces are the only part of ourselves that, in this culture, we can allow to be naked. Odd, since it is our faces that are so diverse and intimate. Our masks give us unconscious permission to commit acts of emotional suicide and self-abnegation. Removing masks is the first step toward taking responsibility for our acts and our lives and leaving the masquerade party of limited beliefs. It is also a foolproof method of discovering your original face.

Keep a Dream Journal

Taoist writer Chuang-Tzu said that he had a dream that he was a butterfly, but that upon awakening, he wasn't so sure that maybe he wasn't now a butterfly dreaming he was a man.

Keep a dream journal. Who you're supposed to be is often completely turned upside down in your dreams. They most often aren't very normal, are they? Write down your dreams as soon as you wake, even in the middle of the night; especially in the middle of the night. Don't edit, self-censor, or worry about grammar, spelling, and so forth. You don't have to show this to anyone.

The dreams fade fast so you've got to capture them fast, using your journal like a Polaroid. Snap! Gotcha! Read them over periodically as you would a novel and you'll discover a whole other life you've been living.

Who are you now? Who are you becoming? Perhaps the relationship of Chuang-Tzu to the butterfly was the same as a caterpillar's. Perhaps, we, too, can evolve toward our destiny through dreaming. Try to do this tonight.

Be in Other People's Dreams

You know those nights when you think you don't dream, or that you can't remember your dreams? Performance artist Laurie Anderson says that's because you're in someone else's dream that night. People were convicted and burned as witches for the same offense in the good old days.

These are modern times, so fear not.

Your razor: Whose dream would you like to be in tonight? Try it out by thinking about this before you drift off to sleep tonight.

Sleep Your Way to Success

An Hasidic rabbi told one of his students to switch the normal direction of his sleeping as a spiritual exercise.

The razor: Try sleeping with your head at the foot of the bed tonight. How does it feel? How much resistance do you feel from your habits and beliefs about how things should be normally done? Are your dreams any different? Your waking life? Wake up from limiting, normal beliefs by sleeping abnormally without limits! Try this for at least one night.

Normal Car Behavior

Have you ever been stopped at a light in traffic and looked over at the person in the car next to you? Invariably, they're picking their nose, singing along with the radio, or admiring themselves in the mirror. As soon as they see you looking their way, they stop whatever they were doing, and assume "normal" motor vehicle operator form, both hands on the wheel, back straight, and eyes unblinkingly staring ahead, strictly business. This has happened to you, as well, as the "victim" of an unwanted and curious audience.

Why is it that we stop our very human behavior when observed? What cultural imperative are we fulfilling in acting embarrassed when observed? We all check each other out as we pass on the highway, somehow relieved that, yes, there are other people in those metal boxes. We, as humans, are relentlessly curious about how others behave and act in their private moments, gaining confirmation and affirmation that we aren't so weird (or abnormal) ourselves.

The razor: Next time you look at people in a car or they look at you, acknowledge them with more than a sly glance. Smile and wave. Next time you catch someone singing, primping, or picking, smile and do the same, letting them know it's not such an awful thing to be human. Next time you're caught doing these things, just shrug in resignation and smile.

The Tree of Belief

Be a belief genealogist. Draw a family tree going back as far as you can and as far forward as well, to your children, friends you influence, etc. Try to trace the beliefs you inherited from your parents, ethnic culture, family religion, etc.

Instead of just simply naming the relatives and ancestors, name them also by the belief or emotional state you've inherited. How far back does it go? How far into the future are you willing to allow it to continue? How much a product of your "accidental" genetic and emotional ancestry are you, as opposed to your imagined "free will" about these things? Are you who you're "supposed" to be? Doing this belief tree, you can actually see the "accident" in progress and identify areas of your life that need deliberate attention, perhaps even pruning.

Your Secret Name

In the Kabbalistic tradition, Hebrew letters of a word are sometimes scrambled to see what is revealed. Letters and numbers are understood to have spiritual correspondences and hidden meanings. Someone in one of my workshops pointed out that my name, Mel Ash, spelled backwards, Hsalem, could be construed as Shalom, or Peace (would that it were so!).

Take the letters of your own name and rearrange them until you, too, get your secret name and quality revealed to you. What's in a name? Find out. Is your name a virus, an accident? Is unscrambling your name the vaccine?

Shuffling the letters of your name will rearrange your sense of solidity of self and perhaps give you the freedom to unscramble other areas of your life, revealing hidden meanings. Your given name may *appear* normal. Your secret one needn't.

What's in a Name?

This is the famous question posed by Shakespeare. The Lakota answered him. Native children were given temporary names until they grew up a bit. Then they received appropriate names based on their unique attributes. This seems a dignified and sane

way of naming, since the very act of naming is fraught with power and significance.

In some cultures, knowing someone's name is to exert power over them, so people often give a public and more superficial name. How much of a slave are we to our names? What expectations were we saddled with along with the syllables? What family, ethnic, or religious traditions and accidental beliefs are we unwittingly, and often unwillingly, carrying on?

What "normal" associations and expectations come along with our handles? Does being named "Bobby" or "Becky" determine our normality as much as "Maynard" or "Mabel"? One of my self-created names in the past was "Melvis," and it was by this name that I was known when I was art director at a music newspaper.

Give yourself your *own* name, based upon your deepest longings and hopes and talents and skills. Make sure it reflects your true qualities, even if the reflection is only in the sound the syllables make on your tongue. Reveal it to close friends and family and perhaps ask them to do this exercise as well. You could use these names in personal letters, phone calls, and meetings.

Switch Sexes!

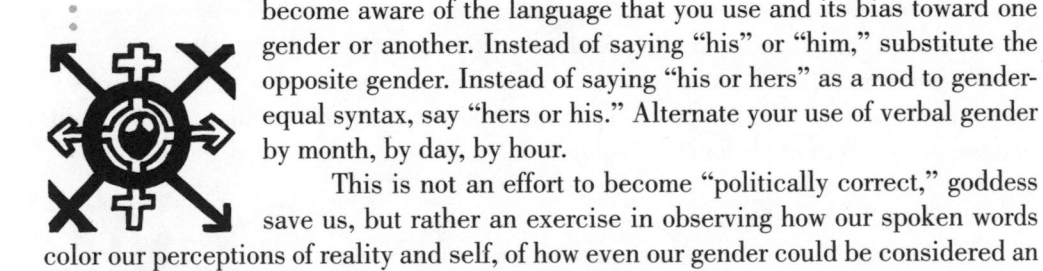

No, you don't have to undergo surgery for this one. Simply start to become aware of the language that you use and its bias toward one gender or another. Instead of saying "his" or "him," substitute the opposite gender. Instead of saying "his or hers" as a nod to gender-equal syntax, say "hers or his." Alternate your use of verbal gender by month, by day, by hour.

This is not an effort to become "politically correct," goddess save us, but rather an exercise in observing how our spoken words color our perceptions of reality and self, of how even our gender could be considered an accidental point of view, a crapshoot of chromosomes.

If you try this even a bit, you'll discover deeply entrenched habits and resistance and begin to transcend limiting verbal beliefs about who we're supposed to be.

A razor: Write a paragraph about yourself in the third person, but referring to yourself by the opposite sex.

Repent Your Normal Behavior

Henry David Thoreau said, "The greater part of what my neighbors call good I believe in my soul to be bad, and if I repent of anything, it is very likely to be my good behavior."

The razor: Can you identify any of your neighbors' behaviors (local, national, global) that you consider to be "bad," yet they themselves and society at large consider "normal" and "good"? What, of your own beliefs and behaviors, secret, repressed, or overt, do you consider "good" but would be viewed as antisocial or abnormal by the general consensus and mass hallucination masquerading as "reality"? What "good," "normal" (conforming, untrue to self) behaviors would you repent of and change if you could? Make a list of three repentances for starters.

We Are Family

Kurt Vonnegut has several recurring themes in his body of work. One of the themes he continually examines is that of belonging to an extended family, or "folk society" as he calls it. He believes a lack of voluntary membership in a larger group of like-minded individuals to be one of the main problems of contemporary society. He advises that one join lots of organizations, even if they're comprised of "idiots." Some of his stories involve the creation of "artificial" extended families based on the random assigning of commonly held middle names.

What extended families do you belong to? What like-minded folk societies help you become *who you really are* and not *who you're supposed to be?*

This example from Bob Kerr's *Providence Journal* column of December 27, 1993: Mr. Kerr interviews members of two "secret" men's clubs in Providence: the Tuxedo Club and the Polynesian Kings, whose memberships are in the low double digits, he says. Says one King of his group, "The Polynesian Kings are top secret. But no one has any interest in us. Each Polynesian King is the honorary king of a different island. They're very spiritual, back-to-the-earth: beer, poker. They're mostly bachelors, lonely single men. They get back to masculine communal roots."

Asked about how to become a member, he says to forget it: "If it's meant to happen, it will happen. But we encourage others to create their own tribal groups."

Another razor: Create your own extended tribal group based around a common interest, say chess, S&M, or even working the exercises in this book. Meet regularly. If this is impossible to actually do, what sort of group would you like to belong to?

You Mother, You!

Tibetan Buddhists believe that we've all been reincarnated so many countless times that there's a good chance that we've each been every other's mother in a previous lifetime. *Who we're supposed to be is in large part dependent upon who we believe our parents are.* This razor is a way of enlarging limited ideas about your choices in whose child you are, were, or could be.

Tibetans keep this exercise constantly in mind as it generates compassion for each being they encounter, thinking: At some point, this being, no matter how loathsome to me now, was my very own nurturing mother. You could try to adopt this attitude as well.

The razor: Next time someone is giving you a hard time or making you uncomfortable, try really hard to see them as your mother. Now when someone refers to you as a mother, instead of getting angry, smile and thank them. They're a mother, too!

Acting Fishy

The native people of North America didn't really distinguish between "art" and "real life" or between "normal" and the "abnormal." They lacked these alienating beliefs about divisions and life.

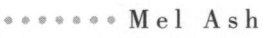

Here are what are called "Events" adapted from *Shaking the Pumpkin* by Jerome Rothenberg, a collection of Native North American poetry. These examples are "poetry in motion," and you might try them as razors to explore what constitutes "normal" behavior.

Better yet, write and act out your own, challenging and transcending beliefs about who you think you are! These events work best with a few friends or family.

(Iroquois) Dream Event I: After having a dream, let someone else guess what it was. Then have everyone act it out together.

(Iroquois) Dream Event II: Have participants run around the house, acting out their dreams and demanding that others guess and satisfy them.

Dakota Fish Event: Four or five people lie down and imitate a fish out of water.

Kwakiutl Gift Event: Give everyone a new name. Pretend to be different things.

Eskimo Vision Event: Go to a lonely place and rub a stone in a circle for hours and days on end.

Crow Crazy Dog Event: Talk crosswise, say the opposite of what you mean, and make others say the opposite of what they mean in return.

Navajo Language Event: Hold a conversation in which everything refers to water. If someone comes in the room, say, "Someone's floating in." If somebody sits down, say, "It looks like someone just stopped floating."

Fire!

Buddha said that life is like a house afire and that the people inside are sleeping, dreaming. One good way to wake up is to pretend that your place actually is on fire. You've thought about this one as well, I'm sure. If your place was on fire, what would you save? This is assuming, of course, that family, animals, etc. are already safely out.

You may save one thing and one thing only. What is that thing that you would save? Think deeply on this. This object is who you're supposed to be.

A book? A photo album? A record? A picture? What? This thing is the material representation of your current state and what gives meaning to your life. What does it mean? Ask others this question as well.

Spend Time with Another Species

Years ago, I lived for a while in the Florida Keys and became friends with a dolphin trainer. I got to spend a lot of time with them in their lagoon. They set the psychological rules and defined the sometimes alien games we would play. The experience transformed me incredibly, shocking my mind into a concrete awareness that human consciousness and belief is only one style of being in the universe, that who we're supposed to be could easily have taken a different shape, say, one with fins. What is "normal" behavior for us is by no means the "norm" for other species.

We needn't travel to other planets to meet incredible and gracefully adapted beings. They surround you! These days, I spend a lot of time visiting my sons' gerbils, just watching them, attempting to chatter and chirp with them: in other words, learning about another view of the world through their unique culture and perceptions, attempting to drop my beliefs about them as "pets" or as "cute," etc.

Think about the beings accessible to you who could become furry teachers, feathered gurus, and finned friends. Spend some time with them, playing by their rules.

The Shape We're In

Write your thoughts, poetry, prose, confessions, ravings, whatever, in the shape that they are, in the form known as "concrete poetry." We put everything in a linear left-to-right fashion when writing or viewing, seeing even history, progress, and our lives, thoughts, and beliefs in this fashion, as somehow moving inexorably from here to there in a straight line.

When we discover that these things usually form their own "organic" self-describing shapes, we are surprised. Writing "concretely" helps to expose the shape that we are really in, accidental or not.

For starters, try writing a description of a tree in the shape of a tree. Then maybe a sad memory in the shape of a teardrop. Have someone trace your profile from your shadow on the wall and inside of it write a description of your current emotional state and belief system that makes you the shape that is you. (For an example, see the funnel-shaped prose in the later section "The Construction of Consciousness.") Conform to your real contours. Who we are supposed to be can be altered and poured into a shape of our own choosing. Shape up or ship out!

Seek Coincidences

If our lives are lived "accidentally," perhaps the antidote is to live them "coincidentally." Carl Jung wrote extensively about the concept of "synchronicity," or the meaning of what we usually shrug off as coincidence. Are we missing vital clues in this mystery of life as we stumble over the dead bodies of our spiritual crimes? If we are the world's way of experiencing itself, then it would make sense that, through coincidence, we are sending ourselves messages all the time, ones that our rigid belief systems and jealous brains reject.

We've all had eerie experiences with this. As I was driving one day, absorbed in thinking about a decision, I literally asked myself aloud, "Should I do it?" Just then a huge Nike billboard caught my eye. It said in six-foot-tall neon letters, JUST DO IT! Guess what? I did it. Who was I to argue with the universe? Or you're talking to somebody and as you are saying or thinking some phrase, the identical phrase is heard on the radio in the background.

Beat author William S. Burroughs has this to say about that in his book *Painting and Guns:* "To me the ultimate scientific fabrication or fraud is Cause and Effect. The key is synchronicity rather than cause and effect. For example, I was thinking about New Mexico, came to a corner—this is in New York—when I turned the corner, there was a New Mexico license plate: 'New Mexico—Land of Enchantment.' I didn't think for a minute that I caused it to be there. But I was thinking about it because I was going to see it in just a few seconds. There was a synchronicity to what I was thinking about and what was happening around me. . . . And now science is saying there cannot be any possible relation between what you think and what you see—between you, my thought, and what I can see in so-called reality."

Your razor: This week, become aware of any eerie "coincidences." Try to find at least one that has personal import. Discuss this with other people. You'll hear some amazing stories.

Hold Up Your Hand

The razor: Have someone else read this to you as you follow the instructions. (This exercise is compliments of my friend Rev. Tom Ahlburn.)

Hold up your hand. Either the right or the left. Let the palm and fingers be at ease. Rotate your hand around a bit—look at it from a number of different angles. Feel the surface of the skin, feel the subtle, pleasurable sensation of touch as your hand moves gently in the air.

It is all very natural, stress-free, just how-it-is. Close your eyes for a minute. Keep relaxing. Can you tell where your hand begins and where it ends? Not really. If you stay open and naturally relaxed, you are still aware of your hand, but you can also feel that your hand is continuous with the space around it. Your hand is not really defined by its skin envelope or by any absolute boundaries that separate it from its environment.

Now curl your fingers into a fist. Squeeze it tight. Hold it. Keep holding it tight. Count to ten—keep holding it. The longer you hold it, the more stressful the effort to keep your hand all knotted up is. It even hurts. If you keep holding it, the curling action actually changes your perception of your hand.

You start to think you have a fist—that a fist is a natural part of your body, rather than the result of something you did to your hand. Keep holding it. If you keep observing how this action changes your perception, you can also notice that your hand (when it is in a fist) doesn't feel continuous with the world around it anymore. It feels much more highly defined, much more distinct and separated out from its environment. You can even start to sense, if you hold your hand in the fist long enough, that it seems as though there is a "center" to the fist, something inside.

Now let go. Relax your hand. First, you notice there is nothing inside, nothing to clench our beings around. Then, if you have been holding your fist long enough and tight enough, you will notice that you can't relax your hand. The muscles are habituated to being in a cramp. They are used to being contracted in a fist. It takes a few moments of intentional relaxation before your hand can return to its natural state of openness.

> When action grows unprofitable, gather information; when information grows unprofitable, sleep.
> —Ursula K. LeGuin

Why did I ask you to do this exercise? I did it to suggest that maybe the answer or breakthrough we are all looking for is—if you will pardon the pun—very close at hand. I think breaking down and breaking through is very much like opening and closing one's hand; it's more than a perfect metaphor for what is always going on in our lives, that this is what is always going on in us.

We are always avoiding reality by contracting away from it, by separating ourselves from others, arguing with them and ourselves about our tight, painful beliefs, cherishing ourselves as the only reality that counts. On the other hand, spirituality is the open hand. In the end, opening one's being is almost as simple as opening or relaxing one's hand.

Put Your Hands Over Your Own Eyes

Say to yourself, "Guess who?" Don't remove your hands until you guess. Be honest even if you get frustrated or angry. Surprise yourself? Please do this right now, before reading any further. If you guessed, you may proceed to the Second Shave.

Alienation and rootlessness,
if we will only understand
them aright, make it easier
to live in our time.

—Hannah Arendt

Second SHAVE

Who We're Told to Be

Who are we told to be?
And perhaps more importantly:
How are we told to be this way?

As we learn who we're
supposed to be,
we begin to shut out any other possibilities or ways of being.
Who we're told to be becomes a closed circle of self-assured belief
and limited, controlled knowledge.

Who are we told to be?:
Who we're supposed to be!
No more and no less.

We know it and we learn to like it.
And we don't want to know any more.

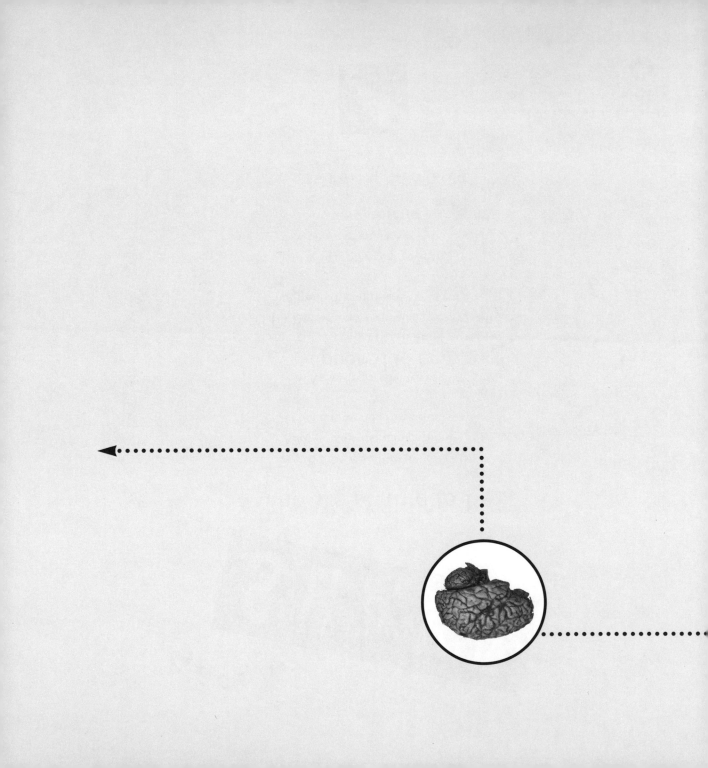

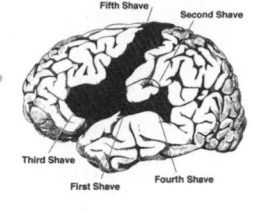

I LIKE WHAT I KNOW AND I KNOW WHAT I LIKE

As information technology has increased, so too has the means of controlling and tailoring it. Coupled with the sciences of psychology and marketing, the decentralizing of knowledge sometimes becomes, if possible, responsible for a centralization of beliefs and limits on a previously unprecedented mass scale.

While there may seem to be an infinity of choices and unlimited access to the information that shapes our beliefs about self and world, upon closer examination we can see just an expansion and sophistication of propaganda techniques, all aimed at perpetuating a very narrow band of beliefs and cultural points of view.

Like the person who wants to be scratched where they itch and only made to feel comfortable, so too are we, as we become ripe for the harvest of the modern belief farmers. Rather than supplying us with knowledge that might possibly challenge and change us, we are subjected to a steady dict of pabulum that serves only to tell us *who we are* and reinforce *who we're supposed to be.*

The Lowest Common Denominator

Through the use of "focus groups"—randomly selected groups of people—business, media, and state can accurately determine the sales and/or aversion potential of everything from covers of magazines and books to their content. If the "focus group" registers disapproval for the idea presented, it is jettisoned and a more acceptable one put in its place, one that will meet with the widest possible approval and sales.

After all, no matter what the "product" is, it is beliefs that we are being sold, a belief that we will somehow be better looking, happier, more "normal," or even superior. Likewise, the absence of alternative ideas or value systems lends support to the belief that these are essentially worthless, marginal, and not worthy of the slightest consideration.

Thus is knowledge dragged down to the lowest possible common denominator, and we are deprived of the right to knowledge that might conceivably challenge and even outrage us. This sort of knowledge, regarded as "fringe" or "abnormal" by the "focus groups" and random opinion polling of shoppers in malls, is often the only knowledge that we truly have a need to know.

It is the unfamiliar quality of abnormal, "unfocused" information that causes us to itch and become uncomfortable in our smug assumptions. We learn to scratch ourselves rather than look for comfort from outside. Confronted with ideas outside our conditioning, we are on the road to freedom. We can use this knowledge as the foundation for a new mode of questioning and perception.

Propaganda serves more to justify ourselves than to convince others; and the more reason we have to feel guilty, the more fervent our propaganda.

—Eric Hoffer

Tell Them What They Already Know

Increasingly, knowledge and beliefs are "market driven," that is, determined by how well they will sell or be perceived. Ideas and information that challenge or call into question prevailing beliefs are deemed uncommercial and therefore not worthy of being valued as a commodity.

Tell people what they already know, sell them what they're already ready to buy. Put it in shinier packages with new names. But never, ever challenge their beliefs about their world and themselves. After all, they like what they know and they know what they like. And they don't like to know anything else.

Thus political philosophy and debate concerning life and death issues can be reduced to sound-bites and feel-good clichés. Religious illumination is enfeebled to the defensive flickering of institutional candles surrounded by the darkness of the unrighteous. Emotional propaganda is rendered in a pop shorthand of self-esteem and self-empowerment with little or no thought given to which self we're talking about esteeming or empowering here: the false one created and manipulated by bland and safe information or the true self, spoken and hinted at in all the great traditions.

Subversion Subverted

What started as subversive activities and beliefs, such as Christianity, Protestantism, and American democracy, are today taken for granted as the established order. One has to wonder: How would these challenges and new forms of knowledge have fared in a "focus group" of today or fared in a poll of "average" Americans, comprised primarily of individuals themselves already conditioned and even brainwashed by the results of yet other focus groups? Would these ideas about justice, freedom, and self-liberation have had a fighting chance? Unlikely. Not sexy and sensational enough.

Bad enough that we are already taught to unconsciously filter out and reject any information or beliefs that offend or challenge our opinions. We've learned how to do this in a thousand unspoken and subtle ways, learning what is accepted and what is beyond the pale. How much more insidious the refinement and further honing of information technologies to further sample and statistically enslave us.

Because of the pervasiveness of the beliefs being disseminated through the culture and our skulls, we come to accept certain things as normal and certain things as not. Having done this, it becomes that much easier to demonize or reject other possibilities out of hand. Our obsessions with personalities and glossy, tabloid treatment of issues have cheapened and degraded the very tool which we must use to do our human jobs: our discriminating awareness.

We become ever more ready to accept substitutes of experience for experience itself and the opinions of others as our own. Our awareness becomes skin deep and our skulls fill up with two-dimensional concepts and second-hand gods. We are scared to death that we are not thinking approved thoughts or acting in a "conventional" fashion.

Even our rebellion is coldly calculated, packaged, neutered, and sold back to us by the forces of the marketplace as fashion or packaged music: rebellion as a fad, "alternative" a code word for a niche market.

Authenticity Has No Bar Code

Any system that honestly discusses liberation and the attainment of true self insists that we de-hypnotize ourselves from the known, from the relent-

> No Utopia can ever give satisfaction to everyone, all the time. And even when the external world has granted all it can, there still remain the searchings of the mind and the longings of the heart.
>
> —Arthur C. Clarke

> Man loves what is vain and dead.
>
> —Jean Arp

less propaganda both within and without. Only by obtaining some degree of emptiness and silence can we even begin to hear the murmuring of our true nature, like an underground spring over which has been erected a Babel of superficiality and despair.

True authenticity has no name, no motto, no logo. True self and happiness are not available or purchasable in this new cacophonous marketplace that drowns out our deepest impulses with feelings of shame and guilt about becoming who we truly are. True self conforms only to its own secret contours, normal or not. The denial and suppression of true self is one of the sources of our shame and pain as we seek the anesthesia of anonymity in the herd.

Becoming one of the faceless many, we are told we are becoming "ourselves" and that we are happy. Still, something gnaws away at our spirits. Some emptiness within beckons us, unsatisfied with the findings of focus groups, polls, and market-driven ideas.

There is no way you can be sold what you already possess unless you willingly allow it, and we do allow it. Personal growth, spiritual liberation, and true empowerment cannot be placed on a charge card or obtained in easy installments. They are rarely sexy, glossy, painless, or fun. The way we change and become our true selves is through experiences that cause us to wake up a bit and question our lives and assumptions, in the spirit of Thoreau's statement, "an unexamined life is not worth living."

Peak and Bottom: Two Paths to the Same Place

These transformative experiences are variously called "peak" by psychologist Abraham Maslow and "ego deflation" or "bottoming out" by the Twelve Step programs. Peak experiences are often precipitated by new and often uncomfortable information entering our lives. Often subconsciously, new ideas seed themselves and take root in the fertile soil of the dormant true self, always hopeful for an end of the spiritual deep freeze.

The experiences can be an ecstatic peak, traumatic and despairing bottoms or, even occasionally, absolutely mundane and commonplace experiences that for some reason trigger the transformative change and awakening.

In *The Transformation*, George Leonard beautifully describes some of the less dramatic ways in which we are reminded of our original natures and start to wake up from harmful belief systems:

It may begin with the fragment of a poem, a few notes on a flute, the distant voice of drums, the silence that follows a koan, the softness of a lover's mouth, an unforeseen glimpse of fig leaves unfurling from the tip of a wintry twig like a flower from a magician's wand, the fatal billow of thunder clouds, the smell of summer rain or autumn smoke. These or less than these (a day of joyful indulgence or denial) may trigger vibrations in some lost and forgotten region of our being, vibrations which can expand and set off sympathetic tremors throughout all of what we term body, mind, and senses. And for a time we are free of the hypnosis. We are wide-awake and tingling, available to an unfamiliar kind of knowing by direct experience.

Spiritual Anarchy and Interior Police

All of this is not to say that alternative information, knowledge, and means of shaving the inside of one's skull are not available. They are, in reality, more readily available than ever before. It is just that they are generally marginalized and ignored by the mammoth institutions which control our daily diets of belief.

These new forms and seeds of healthy spiritual anarchy, belief subversion, and "peak experience" facilitators are more easily drowned in a tidal wave of information than censored and condemned; easier these days to simply ignore the prophets than martyr them, far easier indeed to out shout them, easier to label them mad than crucify them.

And should any of the knowledge we need to grow seep through the tightly woven net of monolithic beliefs, we ourselves can be relied upon to censor and police our own rights to self-knowledge; we, unknowingly, become our own oppressors.

> Be very careful about locating good or God, right or wrong, legal or illegal, at your favorite level of consciousness.
>
> —Timothy Leary

Who We're Told to Be Sexually

Indications of this syndrome can be found everywhere. Nowhere, perhaps, are we more insecure and vulnerable in our beliefs than in our views of our sexuality. Quite often a person's attitude toward their sexuality is a

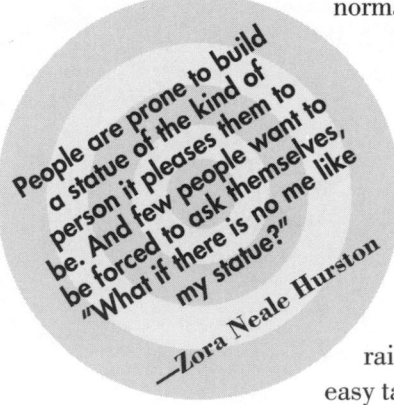

I'm here to drive the money changers out from BETWEEN your temples.

—Bob Black

People are prone to build a statue of the kind of person it pleases them to be. And few people want to be forced to ask themselves, "What if there is no me like my statue?"

—Zora Neale Hurston

fairly good indicator of how the rest of their beliefs will respond as well. If we experience shame, guilt, and self-loathing at this primal level, how can we ever expect to attain happiness at other more easily manipulated levels?

One of the traditional forms of control and suppression of true self by religious, family, and state institutions has been the toxification of sexual self-image. The following is taken from Xaviera Hollander, a sexual advice columnist in *Penthouse* magazine.

The reader might find it incongruous to find such sources in this book. The information we need on our roads to freedom is lurking everywhere, the sharp razors and words for shaving the inside of our skulls already in grasp, quite often in the most unexpected places. Consider Ms. Hollander's words in a much wider context than just sex:

When I am interviewed by the media, the question I am always asked is, "What is the major sexual hang-up of the American people?"

"Normality" is the answer. Like you, they want to know if they are normal. The problem is actually more semantic than sexual. As nobody reads books anymore, all our culture stems from television, where the alternatives to normal are subnormal, abnormal, or, worse still, weird.

We totally forget the other possibilities, like the correct opposite of normal, which is exceptional. I am certainly not normal—I am outstanding.

Everything You Believe Is True

Hollander targets television as one of the main perpetrators of guilt and feelings of abnormality. She correctly identifies the trend toward a narrow interpretation of human behavior and possibility. She puts her finger on the most dangerous impulse we have: to be confirmed in our delusions and told, yes, everything you believe is true, everything you don't believe is therefore abnormal and suspect.

The possibility that we are exceptional rather than weird is never raised. We've been taught that exceptions and outstanding examples are easy targets of suspicion, ridicule, and envy. Every bit as weird and abnormal as we'd suspected all along. According to John Lennon, "They hate you if you're clever and they despise a fool." And so it goes as we are, all of us, dragged down to a numbingly monotonous sameness.

Liking What We Do Not Know

We like what we know and we know what we like. And we don't want to know any more! And so we are constantly sold only what we already believe, never once challenged to grow, to think, to shave the inside of our skulls and become *who we really are.* Instead we are encouraged to lose our true selves in mass fashions, trends, causes, and belief systems usually designed for the financial profit or spiritual power of others.

We are relentlessly told who to be and how to feel about it. Says philosopher Eric Hoffer in *The True Believer,* "Faith in a holy cause is to a considerable extent a substitute for the lost faith in ourselves."

The founder of modern Unitarianism, Rev. William Ellery Channing, upon much the same subject, had this to say:

> I call that mind free which protects itself against the usurpations of society, and which does not cower to human opinion, which refuses to be the slave or tool of the many or of the few, and guards its empire over itself as nobler than the empire of the world.

The work of shaving the inside of one's skull and freeing the mind is to a large degree the work of rebelling against the nearly overwhelming messages and massages we receive daily that only reinforce our comfortable ideas. The work of reclaiming our true selves calls for subversion of our own conditioning and a state of near spiritual anarchy as we shrug off the toxic effects of mass-marketed commodities of normality and belief.

Our true selves *are* exceptional, outstanding, and completely unique. Only by *knowing what we do not like* and *learning to like what we do not*

We are what we do, and above all, what we do to change what we are.

—Ecuadoran graffiti

We invent ourselves out of ingredients we didn't choose, by a process we can't control. It is also possible to uninvent yourself. By a process you can't control.

—Lew Welch

know will we ever learn to truly know and like ourselves. It won't be easy. It won't be painless. But you will have traded generic belief for authentic faith in yourself.

You will really know it. You will truly like it.

Who we're told to be

carries the weight of history behind it.
We may not like it,
but we'd better know it.

Who we're told to be

is no accident,
but rather the purposeful
construction of centuries
of accumulated fear.

Who we're told to be

can be deliberately
deconstructed.

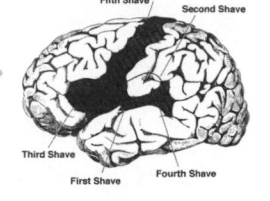

Fifth Shave   Second Shave

Third Shave

First Shave   Fourth Shave

THE CONSTRUCTION OF CONSCIOUSNESS

Have we always been so easily manipulated, so willing to trade our uncertain spiritual freedom for the secure slavery of beliefs? History, as it is written, tells us that this is so, but then again, history is written by the victors, and victory, as we know all too well, belongs to those with frighteningly strong beliefs about what is best for you and me.

Much of the evidence indicates that humankind was not always so dangerously coerced into uniformity. What we take for granted as our consciousness has always been a conditional state, one subject to the sculpting of fashion, technology, and economics. Who we appear to be is no more than the latest model of a long assembly line of consciousness that rolls into our time from the forgotten past.

All that we are, all that we believe, and all with which we limit ourselves is the accumulation of those who have gone before us. We ourselves, each individual one of us, represent the very real crossroads of history. We are handed our limits by the dead hands of the past. We are also handed a ghastly bill which we pay in forfeited possibilities.

What Is Really Real?

We never, as a result of this heritage, consider the possibility that our consciousness is but one of many mdoels available; that what we call "ourselves" and what we call the "other" or "reality" are vague descriptions and social constructions rather than immutable facts. How we perceive and react to "reality" is wholly dependent upon the descriptions of it provided by the slippery concept we call our "consciousness," which is, after all, constructed out of past models and current beliefs. Our means of description, once meant to be tentative, creatively uncertain, and subject to change, solidifies in the face of fear, power, and denial, becoming beliefs.

Beliefs about reality reach out, like mental fingers, to describe what is other, what is not ourselves. These beliefs form a loop of nearly perpetual motion, creating a dysfunctional feedback into the very thing doing the believing and describing: ourselves. We begin to see what we believe we'll see. This circular construction precludes the admission of new or contradictory information that might challenge its "reality."

Single Vision

There are ways out of this closed system that have always been available to us. What we take to be "normal" consciousness these days is in fact a fairly recent constructed phenomenon, according to Theodore Roszak, in *Where the Wasteland Ends.* What we experience through our pervasive belief systems is what he calls "single vision" or the "Reality Principle," an artificial result of narrowed possibilities. The multiplicity of options have been purposely narrowed, he says, until there remains only one single way to perceive and interact with ourselves, others, and the universe.

We all, if dimly, are aware of this "single vision" and what it requires of us. We pay the bill daily and are aware of the payment made only in terms of a vague feeling of "something missing" or a gnawing and usually unspoken lack of fulfillment and purpose. We fill the void mistakenly with the very thing that has created the spiritual vacuum of single vision in the first place: beliefs.

Object or Subject?

The single vision is, in Roszak's view, an objective consciousness, and, according to him and many others, a fairly recent development, at least in its nearly unquestioned ascendency and omnipotence in today's planetary culture. The imposition of this single vision of objectivity is necessary in order to allow the exploitation of the planet and each other, as objects.

Older and more "traditional" cultures interacted with the world in a

> Ego's self-perpetuation is the sacrificial victim, the corpse you stomp upon. As it dies, you are simultaneously cured and live on, transformed, rewired.
> —Anne Waldman

> 1. Never believe totally in anybody else's BS! 2. Never believe totally in your own BS.
> —Robert Anton Wilson
> *BS = Belief System

state of *subjectivity*. The subjective belief system brought human consciousness closer to its environment and others, seeing everything as alive and of inherent, independent worth in and of itself. The objective belief system distances us from one another and, tragically and ultimately, even ourselves. Alienation, a fairly modern condition, is an inevitable result of this way of perception.

Where the subjective belief system might view itself as a *strand* in an interdependent and all-encompassing web, objective belief views itself as an isolated fly trapped in a web of death. To such a point of view, it would seem justifiable to tear that web apart in an effort at "survival," not knowing that it is the web itself and its seamless interconnections that grants and supports consciousness rather than entrapping it.

> We see what we believe rather than believe what we see.
>
> —Alan Watts

Objectivity Necessary for Exploitation

Objectivity arose as a necessary adjunct of the scientific method and the industrial state and was amply justified in the rise of peculiarly Western and Christian worldviews that saw Creator and created as separate, as spider and web, the created forever damned and inherently "sinful." Thus alienated from the source of our being and filled with an existential shame over our very being, it becomes a small matter to alienate ourselves from one another and the planet, viewing them and ourselves ultimately as objects and subject to our manipulation and exploitation, unworthy of sacredness and awe.

God was driven from within ourselves to "Out There," according to Roszak, and squeezed like water from sponges from all other nature, animate and inanimate. The sense of immediacy and subjective vibrancy was driven from the world and with it our sense of membership. A new form of consciousness has been constructed out of new paradigms and technologies.

> The human mind if it is a human mind has not even the habit of being the human mind no of course not.
>
> —Gertrude Stein

"Everything Is Alive and Significant!"

In *Apocalypse*, William S. Burroughs addresses this great watershed of modern history, the line drawn in the sand between the ancient subjective vision and the new objective reality, which has come to straddle the planet with its machines, beliefs, and despair. Says Burroughs:

Mariners sailing close to the shores of Tuscany heard a voice cry out from the hills, the trees and the sky: The great God Pan is dead! Pan, god of panic: the sudden awareness that everything is alive and signficant. The date was December 25, 1 A.D. But Pan lives on in the realm of imagination, in writing and painting and music.

Burroughs points to the birth of Christ as the birth of the modern era of objective belief. The world before Christ, as represented by Pan, was a world in which beliefs were subjective and of a piece with nature itself. "Everything is alive and significant!" was the multiple vision of the day, exclaims Burroughs.

This "Pan wisdom" is akin as well to Eastern and even mystical Jewish and Christian beliefs about the nature of the world, to concepts like enlightenment and gnosis. The real apocalypse, says Burroughs, is when "every man sees what he sees, feels what he feels, hears what he hears. The creatures of all your dreams and nightmares are right here, right now." This awareness is immediate, subjective, and unfiltered by beliefs or interpretations. Everything is significant! Everything is also subjective.

Funnelvision

How do we internalize the toxic belief systems that are the necessary foundations of the monolithic, objective, and suicidal vision that we nonchalantly refer to as the "stress" of modern life? How does our consciousness get in the shape it's in? How do we become who we're told to be?

I myself can understand the near psychosis of objective consciousness only by entering a subjective state and relinquishing the hard sciences of data, proofs, and precedent. This is how it *feels* to me. Instead of considering one's original and newly born self as the "tabula rasa" of the classic psychological cliché, we might instead see ourselves, or rather the shape of our consciousness, as *funnels*.

The top of this original funnel of consciousness is wider than we can possibly remember. It is open and empty in its pregnant and as-yet-unnamed potentialities. Uncritical, unjudging, ready only to receive.

The brain within its groove
Runs evenly and true;
But let a splinter swerve,
'T were easier for you
To put the water back
When floods have slit the hills,
And scooped a turnpike for themselves,
And blotted out the mills!
—Emily Dickinson

Man is made by his belief.
As he believes, so he is.
—Bhagavad-Gita

1. Thou shalt not alter the conscious-ness of thy fellow man.	2. Thou shalt not prevent thy fellow man from altering his own con-sciousness. —Timothy Leary

Into the mouth of the funnel are poured the experiences, events, and information that will form our beliefs about everything. Down, down, down they spiral and push toward the narrow aperture at the end, ready to emerge in a smaller, condensed, and shaped version. The narrowing and organization of the raw stuff of consciousness is perhaps inevitable. What is perhaps not so inevitable is the shape in which it emerges as "us" or as our beliefs about ourselves.

If the narrow spout at the end of the funnel (our awareness) is
perhaps by chance or training not so narrow, more stuff will
squeeze through, providing a bigger and less rigidly
defined belief system and resulting sense of self
and reality. In most cases, however,
our spouts have been painfully
hammered into identical
and narrow shapes. The
stuff that emerges
takes on the
shape of the
spout, or
template,

we've

been

given.

There Is No Way to Be Objective

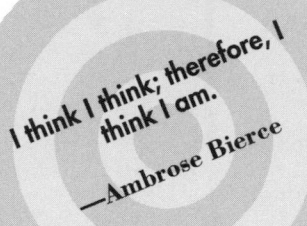

If the spout is star-shaped, then stars we shall be. If it is pinched and tight, so too our approaches to life. Sometimes the spouts are so narrow and constricting that very little original raw stuff can squeeze through unharmed and untwisted. If the spout is so monstrously distorted, is it little wonder that monsters walk the earth, taking control of the raw stuff, distorting and restricting everyone else's spouts of awareness? No wonder to me. Nor to you, either, probably.

Using the hands of our subjective belief and transformative experiences, we can grab hold of our own spouts, stretch them wide, and allow the real stuff of life to come flowing through our awareness in shapes that will surprise, delight, and expand us. Giving up even a tiny bit of our white-knuckled attempts at controlling the funnels of consciousness will yield truly magical results. We can literally reconstruct our consciousness and the lives we will lead.

There's no way for us to be "objective" about all this. It is we ourselves who are the subjects of our experiments and deconstructions in consciousness, not objects. It is we ourselves who by proclaiming the tyranny of single vision can once again peer in wonder at life through many eyes and, looking back at ourselves in subjective surprise, reconstruct the *many* visions that have always been ours. What's yours?

Second Set of

RAZORS

Who we're told to be
reinforces our accidental beliefs
and constructs a limited consciousness.

Acting "crazy," "childish," or "abnormal"
are some of the ways in which we can become
who we really are.
You can begin telling yourself
who you really are
by making some simple changes
and by asking some impolite questions.

Use this second set of razors
to begin constructing
a new consciousness.

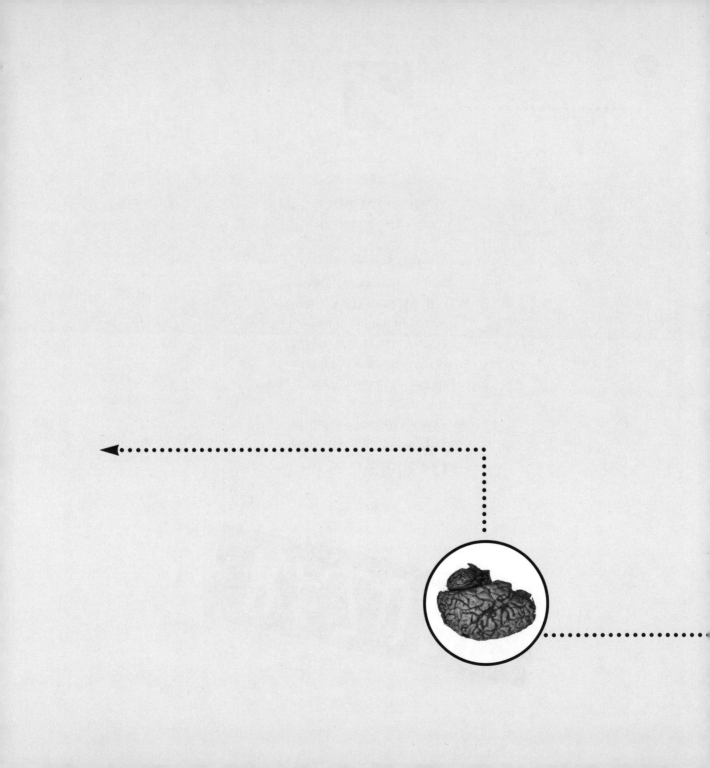

What's Your Vision?

Here is a picture of your "funnel." On the lines inside the funnel write out five descriptions of the "raw stuff" that was crammed down your spout and emerged as the "you" you were told to be; "stuff" that you might be wanting to transcend as limiting beliefs.

At the bottom of the spout, draw a simple shape representing yourself as the product of funnelvision: perhaps a star, perhaps a small, narrow circle, perhaps the outline of a religious symbol.

Beside this symbol, draw another representing the shape to which you aspire as you become who you really are.

1

2

3

4

5

What's Your Single Vision?

Dr. John Lilly presents these directions in *The Dyadic Cyclone* for an exercise he calls "Cyclops": place your forehead and nose directly on a mirror. When you do this, you'll see one "cyclops" eye rather than your own usual two. Now concentrate your attention on the pupil of your cyclop eye. Continue your cyclopean concentration for a couple of minutes in order to confront your beliefs about who you were told to be.

Lilly says that there is nothing esoteric or mystical about "Cyclops" other than what kind of metaprogram (i.e., beliefs, expectations) you bring to it. It is, he says, useful for a kind of "personal spiritual movement."

You can also do this with another person by tilting and touching your foreheads together at the traditional site of the "third eye." Each of you will appear to the other as a Cyclops. Stare into each other's eye for a few moments for the same results as the solo "Cyclops." This is a "single" vision of an empowering sort and radically different from what we usually perceive.

You Are How You Eat

Eat with wooden chopsticks and bowls for a week instead of metal forks and china plates. The entire experience of eating is transformed into a more mindful activity. You can change very simple and usually unquestioned aspects of your life, making subtle and significant differences in the way you were told to do things. Can you list some others?

You Are Who You Eat With

In the Jewish tradition, an extra place is set out at dinner for the unexpected guest as a symbol of generosity, for the Messiah who might show up at any moment without warning.

Doing this every mealtime will begin to affect your awareness of eating, gratitude, and openness. It will construct a new multi-visioned consciousness fraught with mystery and expectancy.

Set an extra place at dinner tonight. Or ask for an extra table setting next time you dine out. And invite a homeless person to come in and share your meal. They might be the hidden Messiah.

You Are Who You Eat

That's right: cannibalism. How many other so-called "spiritual" books even dare to mention this? Not many, I'll betcha. Yes, cannibalism is a fine way to shave the inside of your skull, no matter what you've been told.

On an episode of *Northern Exposure,* the characters have a conversation about who they would eat first amongst their friends if they had to do it in order to survive in a huge blizzard. Much like the horrific experience in the book and movie *Alive,* about a soccer team that crashes in the Andes.

Murder is not involved in this. Your intended meals have already been killed anyway and flash-frozen in the blizzard or crash. Who do you eat first and why? For what type of nutrition: physical, intellectual, emotional, aesthetic, or spiritual? You are, after all, who you eat.

In this exercise, "eating" can also be seen as a metaphor for "influenced by." We consume our friends' influences and beliefs constantly and unconsciously, getting clues about who we're supposed to be and what is considered normal. In this razor, you can choose from the menu.

So . . . who do you eat first and why? Make a list of three people. After their names, list the quality you are consuming. You might be advised not to share the results with your friends, however. That might be in bad taste. Or do share it with them, collaborating on a mutual menu.

You Are What's Eating You

Who we've been told to be eats away at us night and day, making us feel powerless. Yes, you *can* eat away at what's been eating *you!*

The razor: Write the belief or limitation that causes you the most suffering on a small piece of edible paper and eat it. Or write it in syrup on a pancake, with cinnamon on toast, or frosting on a cake. Devour it mindfully and say goodbye. Or simply project the belief mentally into a foodstuff before you eat it. Do this in all seriousness.

There's a guy in Arizona who does something similar. You write down the cares you want taken from you and send it to him with five bucks. He burns it together with all the others he receives and then flies over a real town called "Carefree," scattering the ashes as he flies. So maybe you, too, could write your demon's name on a piece of paper and burn it, scattering the remains in a nice place like Carefree.

You Are How You Drink

Tea ceremony is an old Japanese Zen technique for entering the moment freed of limiting beliefs and investing your life with an unspoken meaning.

Basically, a small group of people are served and drink tea in an aesthetically-pleasing room, with a couple of flowers, a calligraphy scroll, and the pot and teacups themselves. Conversation is restricted to the tea, the implements, the other objects, and the ambiance of the tea-ceremony environment. By discussing only what is happening and the environment in which it is happening, one's attention is forced to focus on the moment and one's part in making it happen.

While this may sound and feel (at first) artificial to many modern people, after a bit of practice it becomes overwhelmingly graceful and stress-free, a lot like the way we imagine life should really be. You learn how to sip and savor life rather than gulping it down without tasting it.

Try this out for yourself. You don't need all the "exotic" equipment. At coffee break, perhaps, just discuss and comment on the aroma and the flavor of the coffee and the cool-looking Greek diner design paper cups. Consider the aesthetics of the calendar hanging behind the counter. Run your fingers lightly over the cool formica of the table. Pay attention to the exquisitely random sounds of silverware, china, and traffic.

Doing this distances you from your beliefs about what you *think* is happening and gives you a way to experience what is *really* happening in what could be called an "expanded present." Reality is telling you who you really are if you can just pay relaxed attention.

Those people who are following you? Pretend they're talent scouts.
—Tom Robbins

Play with Children

From Saint Thérèse of Lisieux, the Little Flower of Jesus: "You are wrong to find fault with this thing and with that, or to try and make everyone see things as you see them. We desire to be 'as little children,' and little children do not know what is best: to them all seems right. Let us imitate their ways. Besides, there is no merit in doing what reason dictates."

St. Thérèse attempted to live out the words of Jesus that in order to enter the kingdom of heaven, we must become like little children. This is really the state without limiting beliefs about "who we're told to be": "Oh, grow up. Stop acting so childish!"

Spend some time playing with children, at least a solid hour of complete immersion in their activities, perhaps on a playground or doing a craft. They understand. They'll show you the entry to the kingdom of heaven.

Play with Yourselves

If you do this as a child, they call you cute. If you do this as an adult, they call you crazy, so let's keep this one our little secret, shall we?

Invent a secret companion who is with you all the time, observing you and not judging. They called this a guardian angel when I was a little kid, but it gave me the creeps to think about it, being assigned this invisible creature from my birth, plus the GA apparently reported everything back to HQ. This is different.

How does your new friend affect your thoughts and behavior? Are you so alone anymore? Try imagining your "shadow" friend for at least a day as you go about your "normal" activities.

In Tibetan Buddhism, a similar technique is prescribed to monks. During meditation, they are taught to visualize small creatures in the form of deities called "yiddams." They pursue this until the visualization appears completely real, even moving and talking. Stories abound about pesky yiddams that followed their creators around after meditation, harassing and embarrassing them and so forth. At the end of the practice, the monk dissolved the yiddam. This was to teach the monk to question

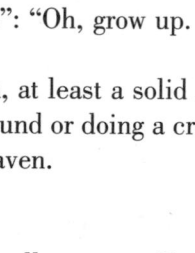

Children are as old as the world, some of them grow younger as they age. They are as those who no longer believe in anything.

—Francis Picabia

what is really real. If he could do *this* with his mind, what else was he believing without his conscious knowledge or assent?

• • • • Talk to Yourselves

Talking to yourself is a sure sign of insanity or money in the bank. So said my grandmother, who had more insanity than money. She never talked to herself so maybe that's the reason. In any event, talk to yourself, foolish as you will feel. We avoid a confrontation with our true self more it seems than with our worst enemies. Remember the words of Pogo: "We have met the enemy and he is us." Use a mirror if you like. Check in with yourself. Challenge yourself. Argue with yourself. Apologize to yourself. And above all, forgive yourself. Do this for at least five minutes to see what it feels like. Go do it now.

Your Life Is an Unwritten Book
Please read the following:

**"Life's Extremely Little and Completely Condensed Instruction Book"
by Rev. Tom Ahlburn, Providence, Rhode Island**

1. Don't go looking.

2. Let go of everything.

3. Be utterly empty.

4. Refuse nothing.

5. Be absolutely honest.

6. Don't ask anything   for yourself.

7. Wait and see what happens.

8. Maybe nothing will.

Books (even and especially *this* one) tell you who to be and form our vision. What would your "Extremely Little and Completely Condensed Instruction Book" read like?

Write out eight short statements summarizing what advice you would give another person, the eight most important lessons you've learned so far. Tell *yourself* how to live.

Your Life Is an Open Book

Old-time Christians came up with something called bibliomancy. This is really like fortune-telling of a sort. Synchronicity, if you're junger than that. This is an excellent razor for attacking the single vision of the written word and letting the book tell you who you really are, not who it wants you to be.

To do it, you let a Bible, Koran, Talmud, or I-Ching fall open and allow your finger to fall at random on a passage. This is a divine message for you!

You could try this as well with the dictionary, newspaper, or any other spiritual book. Uncertain? Confused? In need of direction? Try it out and see how your beliefs about meaning interact with this "random" message you've selected or sent yourself. Try it right now using this book. Then get another one and try it.

Your Place Is Who You Are

Rearrange your stuff regularly. Change the pictures. Move the furniture. Paint the walls different colors. Hang kites and umbrellas from your ceiling. Nail rugs and chairs on your ceiling. I don't care. Where you live is also telling you who you are. Disorient yourself. Reorient yourself. Surprise yourself as you bang into the couch in the middle of the night. Keep yourself on your toes.

Make your living space reflect your evolution. We don't live in museums or a photo spread in *Architectural Digest*. Make your environment challenge, and change who you were told to be. Put up sayings, affirmations, negations, tongue twisters, and side splitters. Combine totally inappropriate styles, eras, and cultures. Haunt yard sales, auctions, and basement shops for artifacts and elements. Make your space a launching pad for your awareness, not a refined and tasteful cell.

A simple razor: Change one aspect of your living space today, perhaps by switching two pieces of furniture or art.

But what will the neighbors think? What they always have. Now they know for sure, that's all.

Your Place Is What You Are

During one of their first meetings, Don Juan, Carlos Castaneda's Yaqui Indian sorcerer and teacher, tells Carlos to find his "place" to sit. Subsequently, Carlos learns that we all have "places" that are friendly to us, our "places of power." I'm sure that you've already sniffed out your place of power, although more intuitively, unconsciously perhaps. (Remember Archie Bunker's famous chair and his outrage whenever anybody else sat there? We all have favorite places and locations where we sit and attempt to go about our being. This is why.)

A razor: Put this book down and examine your level of security in the place where you're sitting right now. After a couple of minutes of this, continue rereading in a different location, one not normally frequented by you. Is there resistance? Or a more secure feeling? Try it out in different rooms as well.

Try this also at work, church, restaurants, wherever. Yes, there is a place for you in this world; a very special place. Where you sit is telling you who you are. Instead, tell yourself where to sit!

Confess, Part 1

"Tell me one good thing you ever did in your life," said the founder of The Church of God the Utterly Indifferent in Kurt Vonnegut's *The Sirens of Titan.*

Go ahead, write down one good thing you ever did in your life. Really. Deeply. Be honest with yourself to the point of tears. Measure the rest of your life by this thing and if it comes up short, be sure to try and do *other* good things.

Half a truth is a whole lie.
—Yiddish proverb

Or to put it another way: What is the best thing you've ever done in your life? Other systems tell you who you are by insisting on other beliefs about "good things," such as promotions, beliefs, and so on. Make up your own standard. Ask other people.

Confess, Part 2

Confess a deep, dark, shameful secret or deed to a total stranger, maybe in a bus or air terminal. Go to confession if you're not Catholic! Go to synagogue and atone all day on Yom Kippur if you're not Jewish! The limits of who we're told to be begin and end with the skeletons we keep in our closets. Confessing and atoning will shave the inside of that skeleton's head!

Confess, Part 3: What Is the One Question You Hope You're Never Asked?

I just asked it . . . your answer? Write out your question and attempt an answer. At the end of this book, return to this razor and see if your responses would differ.

Confess, Part 4: What Is Your Most Secret Sexual Fantasy?

Reveal it to another person you feel safe with, taking the risk that this razor will expand your limits. Make the fantasy happen if it is possible to do so without harming yourself or another. Write it out first in explicit detail and share it with someone. Sexual shame is often the wall between the conditional, belief-infected "you" and your true nature.

Use fantasy fulfillment to batter down those defenses and to remove your psychological armor. If you can make *this* come true, springing to life out of your wildest dreams, what else are you capable of? How thick is the line between fantasy and reality, how real is it really? (In most non-Western spiritual cultures, spiritual and sexual energy are closely entwined, the borderlines between them indistinct and free of guilt.)

> Everything not strictly forbidden is now mandatory.
>
> —Schwa bumper sticker

Examine your beliefs about possibilities, limitations, self-image, and so forth in the light of the experience. What other fantasies do you dare to actually enact? Skydiving? A tattoo?

Confess, Part 5: Tell the Truth

The whole truth and nothing but the truth! I'm sure we all feel we try to do this anyway but we're really just lying to ourselves.

The razor: For a day, try really, even brutally, hard to tell the truth! Call 'em like you see 'em! Even the most "honest" among us tends to exaggerate and embellish unknowingly. Try not to do even this innocuous seeming bit of reality embroidery. Especially to yourself. Especially when you're alone and silent.

Hardest of all not to lie to ourselves. Who knows? You might discover that the truth is what was wanted all along, that it was only your silly beliefs that were lying to you all along. (Warning: This, however, is one of the most potentially dangerous methods in this book.)

That's Not Me!

Remember the first time you heard your voice on a tape recorder? "That doesn't sound like me!" is what you surely exclaimed. I know I did. That's because you hear your own voice from inside its boney amplifier. I'm sure other people who heard the tape agreed that, no, it really did sound like you despite your protests of unrecognition. That may have been the first time your beliefs about your self-image were challenged.

Nowadays, with video equipment nearly ubiquitous, we can fully assault our beliefs about self, although many of us are by now jaded with all this ubiquitous electronic self-reproduction.

The razor: Videotape yourself talking about yourself and watch it as you would a broadcast talk show. What the hell! Interview yourself using two chairs, switching

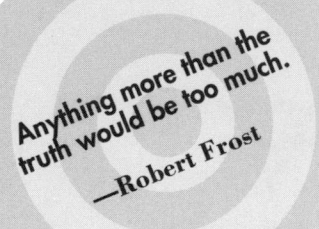

from one to another. As you watch, try to use someone else's eyes and point of view. Ask yourself: Who is this person? How did they get this way? Is that really me?! Yup. Use a tape recorder for the same effect if you don't have access to a video camera. Interview yourself about the subject of normality.

This Is Me?: Get Naked

There is no better or faster way to expose not only ourselves, but also our fears and beliefs about self and who we're told to be, than shedding our uniforms. Naked, we are all essentially equal. I don't think we're as afraid of nudity itself as we are of our lack of protective coloration and cultural camouflage. Without clothes, it's hard to play lawyer, artist, policeman, or whatever role our chosen uniforms dictate; we become simple mammals, something we, in our electronically frenzied way, attempt to deny.

Despite all the overt sexuality in the media, we remain an essentially prudish and voyeuristic culture, deeply ashamed at having been caught in these bodies. To disrobe is an act of immense courage. After a while, it's no big deal and one can get on with examining deadlier and subtler forms of false modesty.

The Shivaite renunciates of India go naked year round. All they wear are their bodies, which are clothing anyway, wearing out as we wear them. Even naked bodies are a form of spiritual modesty, a fleshy flaunting of ownership.

This from a New England nudist camp brochure: "You have nothing to lose but your hang-up. You are going against a lifelong conditioning which became effective when you were about three years of age. Our attitude is that the Creator made no mistakes—and to say a person's body is indecent or obscene shows disrespect to that Creator as well as to the person described."

> One of my correspondents has me convinced that the human race would be saved if the world became one huge nudist colony. I keep thinking how much harder it would be to carry concealed weapons.
>
> —Cyra McFadden

The razor: Spend an entire day nude, with other people. You could do this at a nude beach or a nudist camp. Other possibilities include doing it with friends who are serious about shaving the inside of their skulls. Or you could take off your clothes right now.

What's the Ugliest Part of Your Body?

This is a question posed in a song by the late Frank Zappa. Do you believe one part of your body to be ugly? Why? Where did you get this idea? Is it true? What can you do about it (without surgery)? Draw a picture of the body part you believe to be ugly or deficient. Draw it as you see it in your mind's eye. Compare it to the real thing. Your body image is telling you who to be. Drawing this picture and comparing might tell you something else.

How does this belief about a part of your body affect your other beliefs and resulting self-image? Zappa's answer: "I think it's your mind." (He must have read this book.)

The Rolodex of Change

If you want a vivid example of how the only thing that doesn't change is change itself and of how your own life has evolved despite its seeming sameness, go through your Rolodex or address book of names, addresses, and phone numbers, taking out those no longer current. Count them. How many did you remove? How many remain that haven't changed in five years or more?

Murder

What are the conditions under which you would be willing or able to kill another person? What are the beliefs that would lead you to this act? Can you justify it? Have you even thought about the possibility? List three conditions.

Are there in fact ways that you are already killing people, only more subtly and in the name of something else?

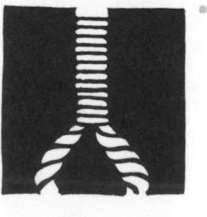

Suicide

What are the conditions under which you'd be willing to die for another person or belief? Again, list three reasons for self-sacrifice.

Are you are already committing a slow suicide? Do you know who or what for?

". . . and what do you do?"

You've heard this a thousand times at parties. What they really mean is "How do you make money?" They could often care less about what you really do. Your money "job" tells them, and you, who you are and places limits on experience.

Attempt to answer this next time by describing those things other than your job that give you life. It might frustrate the questioner, so a certain amount of tact and avoidance is necessary.

"Me? I take my kids to the zoo; I volunteer at my church; I love to read mystery books . . ." whatever. Whatever, in your mind, makes you who you are if your occupation were, for some reason, taken from you. Whatever would be left to hang onto.

The razor: What are those things? Write out five of them.

It's important to stop weighing ourselves against our methods of collecting loose change. In Zen terms: What was your face before you had this job? What is your face after 5 P.M.? Show *this* face.

Loving What You Hate

Expose yourself to something you think you hate or have no interest in whatsoever. Maybe something you've been *told* is worthless or too challenging. I forced myself to listen to opera until I thought I would puke. Now I love it. Cry even at the right times.

What other cool experiences have our beliefs been keeping us from? How small are we really? How big do we dare to get? There's still a lot of time for you to experience this world. It ain't over till the fat lady sings.

Your razor: Listen to a piece of music or read a book that is alien to your belief system and culture. Or see a film you believe you'll probably hate. Or read the next Shave in this book.

The burning conviction that we have a holy duty toward others is often a way of attaching our drowning selves to a passing raft. What looks like giving a hand is often a holding on for dear life.

—Eric Hoffer

Third SHAVE

Who We Think We Are

Who we're supposed to be
and
who we're told to be
becomes
who we think we are.
Who are we really?

The beliefs of who we're supposed to be and
who we're told to be become our means
of self-definition, of self-limitation.
Accidental and "normal" beliefs become a convenient shorthand
for real thinking and experience.

Who do we think we are?
We "think" we are our beliefs and we believe we are our thinking.

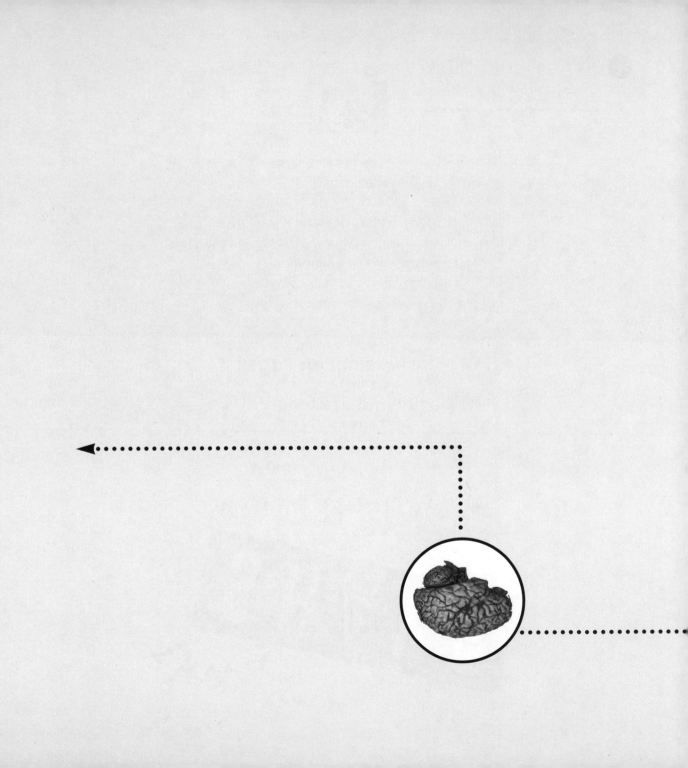

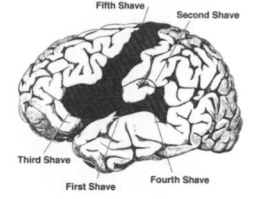

Fifth Shave
Second Shave
Third Shave
First Shave
Fourth Shave

SHRINKING YOUR OWN HEAD:
THE FORMS OF BELIEF

What exactly is this stuff called belief growing between our ears that deadens the sound of the universe and makes us deaf to everything but the whining and whimpering of our own opinions? How can we shave it from the inside of our skulls and exorcise its demonlike possession of our lives? How can we become who we really are and not who we're supposed to be and who we're told to be?

Early on, we are taught to master skills, equipment, and concepts but never, ever let in on the biggest secret of all: the thing that is behind all this doing and being, the machinery of consciousness; our essentially empty and clear minds which exist independent of the sludge of beliefs, opinions, and conditioning that constructs what we call "normal reality."

Reality as a Trophy

It is not reality at all. It is a distorted interpretation of our true natures. We have, through our beliefs, stalked "reality," like headhunters, through the profuse jungle of awareness, severed it from our lives, and shrunken it to a size that no longer threatens us. We hang this dead and shrunken version of "reality" from the boney rafters of our skulls and consciousness, calling it our own and telling daring tales around our small fires of how we acquired this gruesome trophy.

The trophy has become our awareness, our consciousness, our mask, and our blindfold. We become blind to the reality that exists outside the feeble illumination of our campfires of belief.

Some of us hang up diplomas and degrees in place of an actual shrunken head. Some of us have marriage certificates, religious certifications, investment portfolios or maybe just a book or vague set of ideas and expectations on which we erect the "heroic" tale of our lives. No matter. We shrink reality to a size with which we are comfortable and believe ourselves safe and snug through the use of our talismans.

Spiritual Suicide

We are mistaken. The shrunken reality dangling from the rafters of our skulls is not reality at all. It is ourselves whom we have captured, killed, and diminished. It is we ourselves who are denied true life. We have beheaded ourselves and shrunken our own vast potentials. We have, instead of slaying our foe, committed spiritual suicide and called it holy.

That little thing inside your skull, that little shrunken head, if you will, is *you*, and not reality at all. Seeing and experiencing with this shrunken version of yourself, you shrink the entire universe and banish true awakening and potential. Shrunken and dead, this tiny, withered effigy of ourselves inside our skulls and spirits calls the shots from that moment on. This shrunken and dried version of yourself is condensed opinion and belief about reality.

Believing we have become reality's master, we turn our attention to its control and transformation. We want the world to now conform to our little shrunken ideas of how the world should be. After all, didn't we slay our worst enemy? We display their head proudly, defiantly. It is a small thing now to seek to shrink and dry the entire universe so that it matches our own tiny and desiccated spiritual trophies.

We have killed only our true selves and now move as corpses through a land of the dead, calling it life and explaining it smugly with superstitions and rituals we call belief. Whenever we, by extreme chance, happen upon one who still lives, who doesn't shrink her own head, we recoil in fear and loathing, calling them mad or enemy.

Do not put any false heads above your own. The head is the sacred part of your body. Let it do its own work, but do not make any "monkey business" with it.

—Zen Master Senzaki

The less justified a man is in claiming excellence for his own self, the more ready is he to claim all excellence for his nation, his religion, his race, or holy cause.

—Eric Hoffer

Who Am I?

So you can see that rather than mastering the universe and "reality" we have instead left it altogether and entered a one-dimensional world of our own making; a primitive world, really, full of our own superstitions and beliefs. We live in a fantasy and act out a drearily predictable script. Our physical deaths are anticlimactic, really. Something was killed, beheaded, and shrunken a long time before. What is that thing?

It is the thing referred to over and over again as long as there have been humans to ask open-ended questions like, "Who am I? What in the world am I?"

It is the thing that is majestically hinted at in every religion, fleetingly glimpsed out of the corner of philosophy's ancient eye, it is the thing that wraps itself in the brocades and bones of mythology, the thing that writhes helpless on psychology's twilight couch, that howls for recognition in blues and lunges for the throat in art. That thing is You.

> People are becoming increasingly zombie-like. It looks as though their brains have already been removed and they are merely functioning in their spinal cords.
>
> —Jean Baudrillard

The Menu Is not the Meal

All constructed systems of religion, politics, philosophy, art, etc. are the signs of our true selves. They are the maps and metaphors. They do not define the thing but rather refine it. They do not mold it but allow us to hold it.

They are not the thing.

They are not you.

They are all merely art forms, dances, and vague gropings and caresses of you.

Somehow, somewhere, we have confused these symbols of true self with true self itself. We have substituted systems for soul and symbols for spirit. We have abandoned open-ended and vast questions for closed cases. We allow these beliefs to dictate our every emotion and to subvert our deepest longings.

We become sick, angry, lonely, alienated, violent, despairing, disappointed, addicted, and even suicidal, contemplating at last destroying self before system, never once considering that maybe, just maybe, that we are OK

> Have you tried thinking like a shower?
>
> —Chris Stevens, KBHR disc jockey, Northern Exposure

and it is our beliefs that must go. Before we sacrifice ourselves on their altars, either a little bit each day or all at once, we should consider whether in our suicidal lives we are not, instead, the victims of an insidious and exceedingly subtle homicide.

Beliefs Are Homicidal

Our beliefs are *killing us.* Our beliefs are so clever, ingrained, and have become so much a part of ourselves that we believe that it is we who are not measuring up. Our beliefs coax us softly onward in this mad rush to suicide, ladling on guilt and shame.

The fail-safe of belief lies in this dynamic of self-hatred. Feeling we have failed as human beings as measured against our beliefs, we see no other way out than to either kill ourselves literally or to do it more slowly, knuckling under meekly, surrendering our rights as humans, becoming robots of flesh and blood proudly proclaiming our programming far and wide, even seeking to infect others with it so sure are we of its superiority.

What Are Beliefs?

What are these beliefs that steal real life and true reality from us, that diminish and shrink our own skulls, that seek us as willing and gruesome tribal trophies?

Beliefs are basically our tools for interacting with this world. They are no more than *interpretations* of what we experience. They are our tools of awareness. If you had a tool that was broken or hurt you at home, you'd toss it out and get a new one, I'm sure.

Tragically, we don't apply this simple common sense to our most important tools: our beliefs, those tools that we use to interface with reality, those invisible fingers of our minds, which we, like blind people, use to touch and explore experience. Our beliefs instead become the boiling cauldron and potions in which we shrink our skulls. Here are some definitions of beliefs to keep in "mind" as we move together through this work.

Beliefs as Limits

Dr. John Lilly, famed researcher of dolphins and consciousness, has said, in *The Scientist*, "What one believes to be true either *is* true, or *becomes* true in one's mind, within limits to be determined experimentally or experientially. *These limits are beliefs to be transcended.*"

Beliefs are limits we must transcend in order to become fully human and reclaim our right to joy and freedom. The time for experiments has passed. We must transcend through our own hard-won experience or not transcend at all.

Beliefs as Camouflage

Early in life, we don the beliefs and opinions of our environment and culture in an effort to fit in and gain guidance as strangers in a strange land, as groggy victims of an "accident." Very soon, this drapery of belief becomes camouflage. We're afraid of seeing too much ourselves, too "different." We want to appear "normal"; *we want to be told who we are.*

We adopt the herd mentality as the only sure haven from the swirling chaos we've been told lies just outside the small campfire of human consciousness. We huddle and warm ourselves around its feeble illumination, believing ourselves warm and safe.

The process continues until we identify "ourselves" with the very cultural camouflage we've adopted. Our true selves lie hidden in the dense and shadowy foliage of belief deep inside our skulls. Daily, we water and nurture this choking jungle of false belief with our self-loathing, fear, and alienation.

We don parochial-school and Boy-Scout uniforms. We register as Democrats or Republicans. We get circumcised, take a confirmation name, or wear Buddhist robes. Sometimes we even tattoo our beliefs into our flesh: "Born to Lose" on our arms or L-O-V-E and H-A-T-E on our knuckles.

In some strange and talismanic way, we believe in this mad alchemy; that by transforming our exterior forms, such as shaving our skulls like monks,

To be uncertain is uncomfortable, but to be certain is ridiculous.

—Chinese proverb

When a belief becomes more than an instrument, you are lost. You remain lost until you learn what "belief" is really for.

—Indies Shah

or switching the beliefs inside our skulls, we will somehow transform our lives as well, almost as if the dye and fabric of affiliation or disaffiliation will seep magically into our spirits, giving them color and texture.

Nothing to Believe In?

What do we mean by "belief"? Haven't we heard that it is a noble and good thing to "live up to your beliefs," that having "nothing to believe in" is the emptiest form of human morality and surely the slippery slope to nihilism? What *would* we live for? Or better yet, what would we *die* for?

Who we really are dies all the time we are held by belief, either slowly, bit by subtle bit, or all at once. There's nothing wrong with holding beliefs. There's something very wrong when they hold you. There is *Nothing* to be confused about. It is we who are confusion itself and who create out of our thinking and beliefs *Something* to argue about.

Beliefs as Wishes

Alan Watts stated, in his autobiography *In My Own Way,* that the word "belief" stems from the old Anglo-Saxon word *lief,* meaning "to wish." So you can see that the world "belief" itself betrays us. Words and thoughts are the most seductive and dangerous tools of all. Words and thoughts are themselves descended from yet other generations of denial and spiritual legerdemain.

Most people "believe" they know what the word "belief" really means. No question. As Watts shows, however, the word itself, as we normally use it, is not to be "believed." A strict view of the word and its original Anglo-Saxon root would expose our beliefs as mere "wishes."

When we usually think of belief, we imagine it to be immutable and unmovable. Now we discover that the very word we have inherited and use so glibly hinges on vague desires and longings.

> We are the hurdles we leap to be ourselves.
> —Michael McClure

No Aladdin's Lamp

We wish and hope it is so. We know from personal experience that merely wishing does not, in fact, make it so. Beliefs (wishes), contrary to most religions and systems of indoctrination, are not Aladdin's lamps. No genie dwells within the prison of our beliefs waiting to be released by our wishing for a different reality.

We wish it were otherwise. We eventually "believe" it is. The limits of our beliefs/wishes give us a false sense of security and control, almost as if we can manipulate reality like a machine with the control levers of belief and force it to operate according to our hopes and fears.

For a while this approach might appear to work. It works so well that we forget that our beliefs were, after all, only wishes. We actually start to believe in what we have created, genielike, out of wishes and hopes.

> The difference between Heaven and Hell is which end of the pitchfork you're on.
>
> —Rev. Sheldon deWehr

Beliefs as Opinions

The Random House Dictionary defines belief as "an opinion or conviction; a view, tenet or persuasion; an assurance in an alleged fact or body of facts as true or right without positive knowledge or proof."

Beliefs? Look again at the definition. We are "convicted" like the guilty that we are, "persuaded" like the gullible consumers we've always been, and "assured" to sleep like the sheep we've become. All of this without positive knowledge won on our own with our own methods.

Today, we might find a lot of old beliefs laughable and ludicrous. Steadfast and treasured beliefs are usually exposed to be no more than opinions that are muddle-headed, stubborn, and caused by confusion or suffering. But what about us?

Do we find it funny when our beliefs are shown to be shallow or even harmful? Are we able to laugh at our own inflated sense of importance when punctured? Or do we lash out in an anger born of fear and insecurity, desperately clinging to the sinking former lifeboat of our beliefs, not knowing that disillusionment of our beliefs is not drowning?

> If you don't live it, it won't come out your horn.
>
> —Charlie Parker

Disillusionment Is an Opportunity

Rather than using our disillusion as a great opportunity for awakening and change, we usually solidify in our pain and take our suffering as divine proof of our

correctness. Disillusionment carries negative connotations for most of us. When our beliefs are shown to be empty, we say we are "disillusioned."

This is akin to the disbelief that is examined in the section "Beyond Belief" and is not what we have previously thought it to be. Just as disbelief opens our eyes in awe, so too does disillusion strip us of the illusions that our beliefs are constructed as a stand-in for the real world.

It is a healthy and healing process restoring us to our original state of unconditional receptivity, not filtering or rejecting experience as it flows through us and becomes us. It is, ultimately, us and we are it. Everything else is illusion

Equations of Being

Our disillusion need not lead inevitably to gloom and despair. That, too, is another false belief, another spiritually incorrect arithmetic. A + B does not always equal C no matter what we've had drilled into our brains. There are other equations of being that lead to better and more useful sums of experience. This math of spirit is not learned by rote and is not always the same. It is coded in your genes, in your brain stem, and your true self.

When your experience adds up to disillusion, it is an unparalleled opportunity for becoming who we really are. Maybe, just maybe, we can begin to transcend limits we didn't even know existed and enter worlds of life beyond our wildest wishes. All things are possible only at that moment when they all seem impossible, when all the walls of self have been ripped down around us.

Belief Is a Cliff

John Lennon sang, "God is a concept by which we measure our pain." We measure our pain with the yardsticks of our concepts, symbols, and beliefs. Usually, the greater our pain, the greater we desperately clutch to the cliff edge of belief over which we suspend ourselves. What would happen if we simply let go? Death of *who we think we are?* Death of diseased beliefs? Or just maybe more life, a resurrection from the diseased corpse of our old thinking?

Maybe the law of gravity doesn't apply to belief and we would find ourselves floating gently in a state of spontaneity and innocence rather than plummeting to doom if we release our death grip on the cliff of belief. Just maybe it would be OK to relax a little, unclench our teeth, and unchain our spirits.

Unfortunately, we seek this very freedom through the slavery of our beliefs. It is usually when we are clutching the most fearfully to our cliff of belief that we get our hands knocked off by our pain and we fall into disillusion. Most of us land on various ledges and never reach the absolute bottom of this pit of despair. Even on these desolate ledges, we still cling with bloodied fingers and spirits to our rocklike certainty that only doom awaits us below, staring in blank-eyed denial into the dizzying abyss over which we live our lives.

Confront the darkest heart of humanity armed with the rubber sword of humor.

—Ray Zone

Belief Is the Contraction of Fear

It is here that most of us call home and defend most ferociously from those who would tell us of means of possible escape. Even our religions and therapies encourage us to somehow "adjust" to this precarious and untenable position, leaving it up to their "priesthoods" to describe what waits below.

We are put to sleep and lied to. We tell ourselves that we can do no better than to just hang on. Everything else is "crazy," not "normal." We want to be left alone in our fear, which has by now contracted and solidified into belief.

It is only when we propel ourselves over the ledge of self and agree to experience the depth of disillusion that we also experience the freedom that is ours when we are shorn of the beliefs that caused us the pain. Letting go of the contracted state of fearful belief releases an ecstatic expansion of possibility.

Suffering and pushing limits are the very real razors that shave the insides of our skulls, cleaning out the tangled growth of opinions and beliefs that limit us. We learn in a very real way that we have lied to ourselves all our lives; that we've accepted second-place finishes in the human race as the best we could hope for. We dared not hope for more because we'd been led to believe that that was false hope, not what we were *supposed to be or told to be.*

Believing in our true, expansive selves, in *who we really are,* is the only belief we need hold. It is not a belief founded on fears, limits, wishes, accidents, or opinions. It is a belief born of bone and spirit, experience and knowledge. It is true. It is you.

We've learned
who we're supposed to be.
We know
who we've been told to be.
We think we know who we are.

But just where is it
that we store all these beliefs
about diseased and accidental normality?

Where in the world
is the "we"
that does all this believing and thinking?

Are there other ways
to think about who we are
and who we might become?

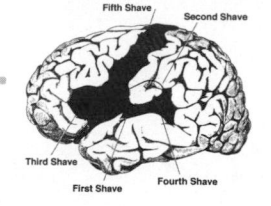

DO-IT-YOURSELF BRAIN SURGERY: MODELS OF CONSCIOUSNESS

Most of us, if asked to identify the location of "ourselves," will point to a place about an inch behind the middle of our eyes. It is from "in there" that we view and direct this show we call "out there." It is from this tiny and unchanging location that we drag the rest of our meat around.

This, in itself, is yet another belief. Many other cultures, primarily native ones with oral traditions, will point to their heart areas. In our cerebral and literate culture, we center our awareness and existential consciousness in the supposed seat of our thinking, in the fleshy and gray wrinkled meat of the "crown of creation": our all-too-human brains.

Recovering alcoholics have a saying: "I'd rather have a frontal lobotomy than a bottle in front of me." We as well, the brains reading this text, might take this folk wisdom to heart, like native cultures. Our beliefs are in many ways the bottles and addictions from which we suffer. In fact, William S. Burroughs considers all beliefs and consumptions to be forms of addiction, varied only in substance or lack thereof, but all just different degrees of the same syndrome.

Like the alcoholic, we might just consider it a good thing to deliberately lose a part of our brain before we pick up and decand some new and lethal form of belief in a vain effort to calm our nerves as they confront a vast and seemingly indifferent universe.

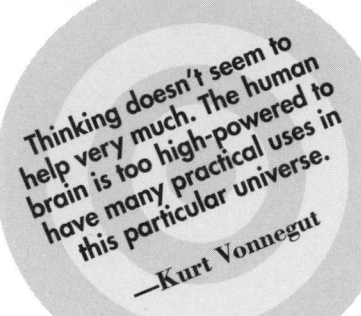

Self-Reliance and Creative Uncertainty

The Transcendentalists of 1840s New England advocated "self-reliance" as the means for attaining true self, do-it-yourself brain surgery and the preferred method of shaving the inside of one's skull. Self-reliance stood firmly apart from the traditional spiritual prescriptions and dogmas, advocating a sort of *creative uncertainty* in the search for personal and universal meaning.

To the charge that this self-reliance would lead to moral anarchy and anchorless spiritual drifting, Ralph Waldo Emerson countered that self-reliance is, in fact, self-trust and a reliance upon intuition or the stirring of the undefinable Universal Spirit within. Therefore, self-trust equaled God-trust. Said Emerson, "There is one spirit through myriad mouths."

The Buddhists call this experience of confronting life without critical judgments or expectations being "set face-to-face with reality." They also use this same phrase to describe a good death experience. Most religions use death metaphors to describe a state of mind that transcends the limits of belief. Christian mysticism would refer to it as the death to self. St. John of the Cross refers to his "dark night of the soul," and yet another Christian writer speaks of entering "the cloud of unknowing."

Unknowing the Known

This unknowing is more than a simple descriptive noun. It is primarily a verb. The process of shaving the insides of our skulls and becoming who we really are consists of relinquishing the beliefs we tightly clench in the white-knuckled fingers of our jealous brains, opening our mental palms and caressing the universe as the beloved, accepting the reality of what our spiritual touch reveals.

We must allow our beliefs about things to die in order to live fully. We can aid in their demise by denying them our attention. We can speed up the process by withholding our responses when our beliefs push the panic buttons of fear, envy, and hatred.

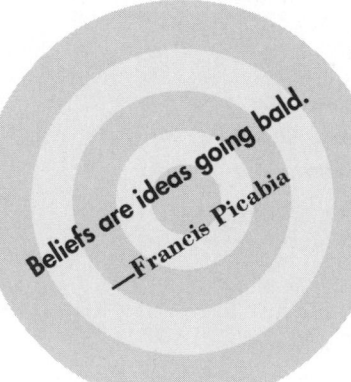

Mind Can Be Colored and Shaped

The nineteenth-century Hindu teacher Ramakrishna once said that the mind is like a piece of white cotton that takes on whatever color it's dipped into. From his insight, we can see that the mind's essential quality remains the same at all times; it only becomes masked and dyed with whatever belief it's exposed to. How transcendent and eternal and divinely "right" can our cherished beliefs really be when tested against Ramakrishna's white cloth. What color is your cloth?

Another metaphor concerning mind involves baking. If you can, for a moment, think of the gray stuff of your brain as cookie dough, undifferentiated and as yet formless, a mass of potential. Our beliefs are the cookie cutters we use to give our brains shape and substance. Our brains can take on any mind-shape depending upon the shape of the cookie cutters of our beliefs.

We usually use only the cookie cutters we are told to use at home, in school, in relationships, and in church. There are other, better ways to shape our brains into friendlier and more delightful shapes. Allen Ginsberg, quoting Jack Kerouac, has said that if the mind is shapely, the art will be shapely. So too the life.

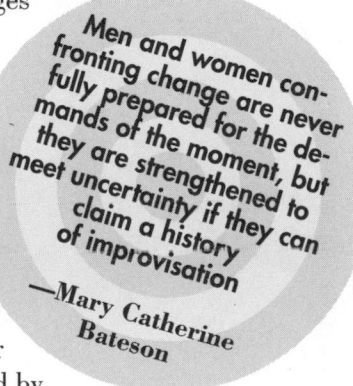

Thought rises to contemplate its own innerness until its power of comprehension is annihilated.

—Azriel of Gerona, Kabbalist (translated by Daniel C. Matt)

Brain as Hardware, Mind as Software

Our brains just *love* to torment us with all their weird electrical charges that we arrogantly refer to as "thoughts" and beliefs. They're just electrical charges arranged in particular patterns really that determine in a very real and tragic way how we will love and hate and respond.

Usually these patterns are set into motion by our parents, schools, and churches, who insist that they are doing us very great favors indeed and that these patterns are in fact "normal."

Dr. John Lilly uses a computer programming metaphor for our situations. Lilly says that basically our brains are the hardware, much like a computer without programming. Our beliefs become the software, as it were, and indeed the operating systems for this hardware. What appears on the monitor and screen of our awareness (and what conditions or programs our subsequent behaviors and reactions) is completely determined by

Men and women confronting change are never fully prepared for the demands of the moment, but they are strengthened to meet uncertainty if they can claim a history of improvisation

—Mary Catherine Bateson

the software we've been sold or stuck with. It simply never occurs to most of us that we can design new "software."

New Software

In order to change the reality we see on the monitor, within ourselves, or before our eyes, we need new software, we need a new operating system. We need, in short, to press delete or clear on our hardware and dump the defective, obsolete, and limiting "software."

In Dr. Lilly's words, which he presents as a meditation exercise, from *The Center of the Cyclone:*

> "Who am I?" Answer: "I am not my body, I am not my brain, I am not my mind; I am not my opinion of me."
> Later this was to be expanded into the more powerful five-part meditation, "I am not the biocomputer. I am not the programmer. I am not the programming. I am not the programmed. I am not the program." When the meditation had progressed to the latter point, I suddenly was able to break loose from the biocomputer, the programmer, the programming, the program, and the programmed and sit aside—from my mind, from my brain, from my body—and watch them operate and exist separately from me.

Limits of Computer/Brain Metaphor

Lilly's brain as "biocomputer" metaphor has penetrated all levels of the culture, popular as well as corporate. In ways Dr. Lilly probably didn't even imagine, the metaphor has come to be used as a nearly unquestioned imperative for us to conform to computer-generated descriptions of reality.

Theodore Roszak, reflecting on this in *The Cult of Information,* says, "The proposition that the mind thinks like a computer is an idea about the mind, one that many philosophers have taken up and debated. And like every idea, this idea also can be *gotten outside of,* looked at from a distance, and called into question. The mind, unlike any computer anyone has ever imagined building, is gifted with the power of irrepressible self-

To arrive at the unknown through the disordering of all the senses, that's the point.
—Arthur Rimbaud

transcendence. It is the greatest of all escape artists, constantly eluding its own efforts at self-comprehension."

The key here, to both Lilly and Roszak, is the transcendent aspect of our minds; it is, dare I say it, the always elusive and slippery *spiritual* component. The brain as computer metaphor is useful when applied loosely and creatively.

We Want to Be Told

Krishnamurti referred to one's programming differently. His definitive work *Freedom from the Known* has this to say about our condition and the questions we need to ask about it: "But we do not ask. We want to be told. One of the most curious things in the structure of our psyche is that we all want to be told because we are the result of the propaganda of ten thousand years. We want to have our thinking confirmed and corroborated by another, whereas to ask a question is to ask it of yourself."

Propaganda and Hypnosis

Propaganda takes many forms: political, social, artistic, musical, sexual, religious, economic, emotional: you name it. Even this book is propaganda for a certain point of view, merely a new program for your biocomputer. The only difference is that it proudly, even brazenly, admits it.

G. I. Gurdjieff used a great metaphor to describe how we are programmed and enslaved with propaganda. He said that the state in which we exist is not a normal sleep but a hypnotized one. He illustrates this with the story of a magician who had a lot of sheep, but didn't want to hire shepherds or erect expensive fences.

He hypnotized his sheep, telling them that they were immortal and would not really die when they were slaughtered, that it was good for them. He hypnotized them also into believing that he was a loving master and that they were not really sheep at all. He hypnotized them into believing they were actually lions, eagles, and even magicians.

They were also hypnotized into believing that they had no need to think about any of these things, that they were absolutely true. As a result, they

> A man is likely to mind his own business when it is worth minding. When it is not, he takes his mind off his own meaningless affairs by minding other people's business.
>
> —Eric Hoffer

> The contemporary hunger for the irrational is always keenest before a cultural dining table offering only the cold and insubstantial leftovers of art and literature.
>
> —Salvador Dali

never ran away, never realized they were really sheep, and were led, like the proverbial lambs, to slaughter.

Mutations of Mind

In *The Dragons of Eden,* Dr. Carl Sagan postulates actual mutations in the brain itself and sees evidence of positive mutations all around us. Sagan says that the incredible intellectual and social conflicts of our era arise from a basic evolution or mutation in our brains, that we are leaving what he regards as the childhood of the species and entering adulthood.

What are the conditions necessary for the brain to take this great leap, to break free of narrow beliefs? Sagan quotes Bertrand Russell to the effect that the development of such a mind requires a childhood period with little or no demands for conformity, and a time when one is encouraged to develop and pursue one's interests, no matter how seemingly abnormal or "useless."

This, of course, is the optimum situation. Most of us were subjected, instead, to repressive systems of conformity and encouraged to follow only "normal" or sanctioned interests, to become who we were told to be. As a result, it becomes nearly impossible to use the repressively programmed brain to free itself. Such a possibility was never entered as data.

Instead, the defensive belief systems of the brain will deny that such a possibility exists. Kurt Vonnegut, commenting on a similar situation, said that dumb people are so dumb that they don't know there's such a thing as being smart. Thus their, and our, sullen and self-imposed limitations.

Two Alternatives

The use of various spiritual disciplines, psychologies, and new technologies promises a lifting of these limitations and a new mutation in human awareness, ways to become *who we really are.* Unfortunately for those of us caught in the brain's double-bind, it seems that the great suffering caused by our beliefs is often the springboard for our ascent.

Only two alternatives are possible: a "safe" surrender to the limits of belief and *who we're told to be* or a risky surrender to the possibility of *who we*

Reality is a crutch for people who can't cope with drugs.
—Lily Tomlin

Confusion is a word we have invented for an order which is not understood.
—Henry Miller

really are, a giving up and relaxing of the lethal beliefs. The latter is the path taken by Zen students who are put face to face with infuriating paradoxes in an effort to force their transcendence. It is the dark night of the soul through which St. John of the Cross passed, emerging in his own spiritual daylight as a religious "mutation."

Religious, mystical, visionary possession states are powerful and wonderful— but they're intimate and precious. They shouldn't be imposed on others.

—Timothy Leary

Four Ways to Change

In *The Aquarian Conspiracy,* Marilyn Ferguson outlines four ways in which our belief systems can change, in which we transform our consciousness and transcend old programs.

Change by exception says, "I'm right, except for——." *Incremental change* says, "I was almost right, but now I'm right." *Pendulum change* says, "I was wrong before, but now I'm right." *Paradigm change* says, "I was partially right before, and now I'm a bit more partially right." In paradigm change we realize that our previous views were only part of the picture and that what we know now is only part of what we'll know later. Change is no longer threatening. It absorbs, enlarges, enriches. The unknown is friendly, interesting territory. Each insight widens the road, making the new stage of travel, the next opening, easier.

Three Forms of Evolution

Charles A. Reich, in *The Greening of America,* identifies three stages of consciousness on its evolutionary journey.

The first stage he calls "Consciousness I." Consciousness I stresses self-repression as well as a cutting off from a larger community. "Consciousness I" uses its beliefs to program itself into a highly isolated and nearly omnipotent ego that confronts what it sees as an essentially unfriendly and hostile world.

In Consciousness II, a belief in the power of organization predominates. II believes that institutions and society are the priority and that the individual must subordinate personal vision to this larger entity. Reich says that

Life is that which—pressingly, persistently, unfailingly, imperially—interrupts.

—Cynthia Ozick

the defining belief of II is that one must "dominate experience rather than being subject to experience."

The foundation of Consciousness III is liberation; that one does not automatically accept goals imposed as "normal" by the larger society. Crucial to III is the freedom to build one's own philosophy, lifestyle, and culture. III is also open to any and all new experience, embracing new points of view and challenging standing beliefs. III is a "state of becoming," considering experience to be the most valuable of all human commodities.

Unhooking Our Brains

However we come to the threshold of this work or whatever model we use as a map is really unimportant. We all arrived here in different ways. As varied as our belief systems are, they remain in one significant way drearily the same: they have enslaved, hypnotized, programmed, and limited us. Our beliefs literally convince us that we are who we think we are, not who we might become.

The ways to becoming are just as varied and, likewise, have an overriding similarity: to use our minds to change our minds, to use our brains to transcend our brains, to deliberately shake off the hypnosis of our accidental belief systems.

In this work, we have to become our own brain surgeons, using scalpels of fearless and objective attention and delighting in the unknown as we shave the inside of our skulls. Our only limits are the beliefs we leave intact.

In ancient Egypt, the brains of mummies were removed by their embalmers with a hook which pulled the gray matter through the nostrils, leaving a body with no disfigurement. Sounds like a pretty gruesome way to shave the inside of your skull, as well as a bit too late and literal.

The point of this work is not to just leave a pretty corpse with lots of toys, but to actually resurrect the walking, talking corpses we have become, our brains hooked to relentless propaganda and beliefs rather than an embalmer's tool. We can perform our own brain surgery while still alive and stop ourselves from solidifying in the embalming fluids of bad beliefs.

Never ask Why What; Always ask What's What. Observe, connect, and do.
—Lew Welch

Learning how to operate a soul figures to take time.
—Timothy Leary

Shaving the Inside of Your Skull

In the workshops that have evolved from creating this book, I use a life-sized plastic skull as a prop. Its concept is similar to Russian nesting dolls. I argue with the skull for a while, ventriloquist-style, moving its jaw, as it attempts to smugly convince me of the "rightness" of its beliefs.

Finally frustrated, I open the cranium like a surgeon, removing the plastic brain. Opening the brain, I remove a computer disc labeled "YOU." I throw the program against the wall. I throw the biocomputer of a brain against the wall.

This disc contains superficial beliefs of "YOU," the macro-programs and infections of politics, race, religion, gender, education, and economics. This is *who you're supposed to be* and *who you're told to be.* The inside of the skull has been shaved, right? The do-it-yourself brain surgery completed and freedom ready to surge into the welcoming cavity?

I again reach into the emptied skull and take out another smaller skull: a deeper level of programming. This skull contains the more intimate levels of insidious beliefs generated by the first level: the micro-programs; beliefs about self-worthlessness, loneliness, fear, dread, impending doom, intimacy, death, love, and so on; the beliefs that make us *who we think we are* and limit *who we might become.* This smaller skull attempts to argue with me in a vain attempt to defend its pathetic and most intimate limits.

Opening that skull, I remove an even smaller brain. Opening that brain, I remove, this time, not a computer disc, but rather another very tiny skull that is solid, unopenable. It has nothing to say to me. On its forehead is a question mark.

Holding it up, I ask, "What is this? Who is this? All our methods of deprogramming, shaving, and awakening have led us to this moment. If you know what this is, you are free. Only you can answer this question." This tiny question mark of a skull is *who we really are.*

I am awake only in what I love and desire to the point of terror.

—Hakim Bey

Conscious faith is freedom. Emotional faith is slavery. Mechanical faith is foolishness.

—Gurdjieff

Losing Our Minds

The work of becoming *who we really are* is a lot like peeling an onion, layer by tearful layer, until finally you arrive at the central reality. How we define it is up to each one of us. Perhaps we will each find a different "original skull" of self at the bottom of all this. Perhaps not.

The entire point of the skull and brain props, of this book, and of all psychotechnologies ultimately is to teach you how to perform spiritual surgery on yourself and become restored to your full uniqueness and original fearlessness. In the words of Esalen therapist Fritz Perls, "We have to lose our minds to come to our senses."

Are you still afraid of losing your "mind," the mind that has been hypnotized, addicted, propagandized, and conditioned into normality and sleep-like submission? Come on! What have you got to lose when you have everything to gain? Do it yourself or don't do it at all. Anything else is senseless.

Third Set of RAZORS

Who we think we are
is determined nearly automatically
by brains and bodies
full of accidental beliefs
and habits of limited being.

Who we really are
can be glimpsed by
deliberately exploring the limits
imposed upon our minds and flesh.

Use this third set of razors to unshrink your head and
reclaim control over something so close
you take it for granted:
your brain and body.

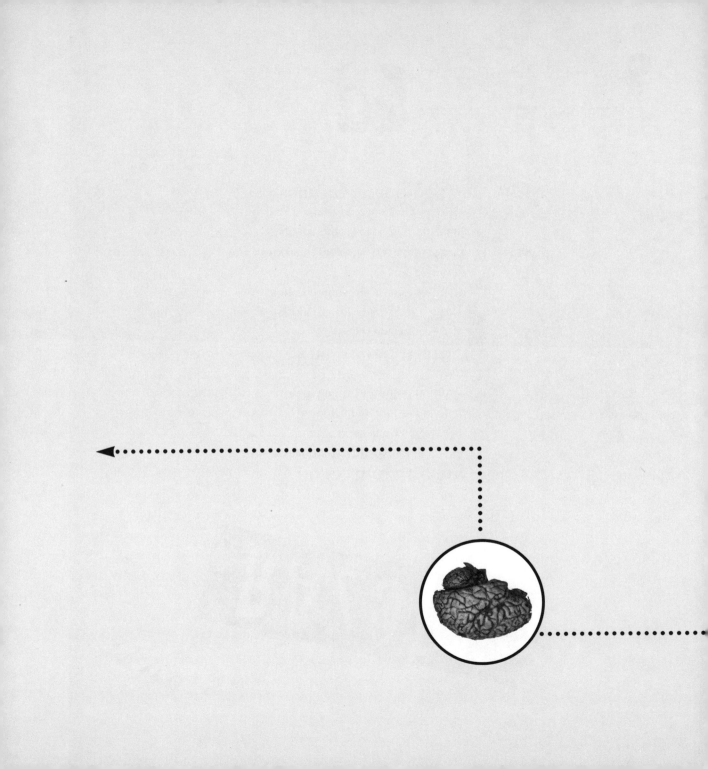

You Are a Robot Run by Beliefs

At least think of yourself this way occasionally. Call yourself "The Robot" using it as the third person, instead of the pronoun "I" or "me." Such as: "The Robot is hungry" or "The Robot is angered by these stimuli," or "The Robot is resisting its programming in this situation." Try this for half an hour.

Doing this will enable you to become an impartial observer of your own belief systems that are running your reactions and behaviors. This robot is typing. This robot is tired. This robot says, "Read the next section."

Your Beliefs Have a Pattern

In the top boxes of the following chart, write in two beliefs you now have. I've filled out the first as an example drawn from my own experience. Work down the chart filling in the factors that led to this belief. It's fairly self-explanatory. Filling in the chart and reflecting on your answers might help you to discover how you ended up the way you are and the process that got you there.

	Belief 1	Belief 2	Belief 3

Zen Buddhism

Belief Formation Factors

1. Behavior
(Experiencing the belief for the first time)

read book on Buddhism when ten years old

2. Identification
(Taking on the beliefs of significant adults)

as a teenager, identified with writers and musicians who spoke about Zen

3. Reinforcement
(Achieving status and acceptance through approval/disapproval of one's actions as a result of the belief)

friends in school thought my belief in Zen was exotic and "cool"

4. Public Affirmation
(Declaring or acting publicly upon one's commitment to the belief)

joined a Zen group, publicly became a Zen Buddhist in ceremony; vegetarianism as a result of Zen beliefs

The Metabelief Game

This activity was devised by Dr. John Lilly in *The Dyadic Cyclone*. Read it carefully and attempt to follow his instructions as best you can.

a) Assume there exist three belief systems, not currently your own.

b) Assume that you have the capacity-ability to believe the reality generated by/in each belief system.

c) Take on belief system no. 1: Believe it totally and ignore any contradicting/paradoxical/disagreeing other belief system.

d) Live out the consequences of belief system no. 1 as true and real.

e) Move out of belief system no. 1 into your usual belief system, your common sense reality beliefs.

f) Take on belief system no. 2, believe it, find the consequences, and return to your own reality.

g) Do the same for belief system no. 3.

h) Examine the consequences, the reality generated by each of the three belief systems, the merits of each.

i) Now specify your own belief system. Call it no. 4.

j) Construct a fifth belief system that includes each of the four previous belief systems. What is your new reality?

k) Can you conceive of a new (no. 6) belief system that includes nos. 1, 2, 3, 4, and 5?

l) Is an infinite set of belief systems appearing? If not, why not? Find a belief that allows for an infinite set of beliefs.

m) What/Where/How is the Unknown? Have you included it in the new/old sets? If not, revise until the Unknown is included.

n) Did the Void appear immediately preceding each of your shifts into the new belief systems during your search? Revise until it does.

Your Beliefs Are Killing You

Purdue University researchers say that people who are regular practitioners of their religious faiths tend to appear healthier than those who aren't. Their *Journal for the Scientific Study of Religion* qualifies this finding, however, with the observation that the "kind" of religion makes a qualitative difference.

The researchers found that people of more "liberal" or tolerant religions and belief systems appear to have the "best" health, relatively speaking. People in religions and belief systems that could be considered more authoritarian and "conservative" have lower levels of "good" health. (The report didn't mention atheists, but maybe none of them have died yet.)

The razor: Can you identify any belief systems you have that contribute to a lessening of the quality of your life and health, some that indeed may become downright fatal? Your beliefs determine not only who you think you are, but who you *were,* as well. Write down at least two unhealthy beliefs. If you can't identify two of your own, then list those of other people.

Your Habits Are, Too

There is an old Japanese saying that no one has less than seven habits. Think about this and write down seven personal habits, no matter how mundane. These habits are your beliefs manifesting in repeating patterns and are, in a very real sense, reflections of who you think you are. Identify seven habits. Make identifying them your eighth.

You Are What You Don't Want to See

Visual addiction is the term artist Robert Williams uses for the "doctrine of retinal supremacy" in his book of the same name. Says Williams, "The eye tastes many flavors, some of which aren't always vanilla."

Williams claims that the eye is amoral and is always drawn to what is "abnormal" or different in contrast to the "normal" and expected, contrary to our moral or aesthetic conditioning, resulting in feelings of guilt and shame.

The eyes are merely doing their job: to look. The brain's beliefs are what interpret the visual stimuli in terms other than what is actually *there,* in terms of good and bad.

You already know this sensation: of telling yourself you won't look at the accident on the highway; you just won't, won't, won't! And then . . . you can't help it. You look as your eyeballs swivel your "unwilling" head toward the scene. The same with nudity. Handicaps. Disease. Flamboyance. Whatever.

Razors for your eyeballs: The next time something like this happens to you, be aware of the friction between the judgment of your brain and the nonjudgment of your eyes. Just look. See what's there without shame or interpretation. Better yet, get a picture of something that repulses you and look at it for at least five minutes.

Force yourself at times to look at things you might consider unappealing, appalling, or disgusting. We see only what we believe, not believe what we see, says Alan Watts. Your eyes believe everything, they refuse nothing. Your visually addicted eyeballs are excellent razors for shaving the inside of your skull.

Who you think you are is revealed by what you attempt to screen out. Who you really are is what you inevitably look at. See?

You Are What You Believe You'll See

This is an exercise Beat writer William S. Burroughs has assigned his writing students as a method of studying their prejudices and perceptions, about what they believe they'll see. Here are the instructions for this razor:

Next time you walk down the street, tell yourself the name of a color, say, Red. As you walk, you'll become aware that all the red objects, lights, clothes, signs, cars, and so forth have advanced from the background that we usually take for granted. Your consciousness will be "Red." Now try it with Yellow, Green, etc.

Do it right now. Close your eyes and think of a color. Look around the area where you're reading this book. What color is your perception?

You can do this as well with types of people, sounds, textures, and whatever you can think up. You are what you see and you can see what you want!

You Are Who You See

Sit across from another person and gaze into their eyes, keeping silent. Give their eyes an optical massage, those compliant tendrils of our souls. Don't do this like a steely stare. Gaze openly, keeping a clear mind. It'll become uncomfortable in a short time. Keep up the looking for at least five minutes and see what happens.

Examine your feelings and fears of exposure and intimacy as you do this. To make it really scary, hold hands. Male dogs regard a look in the eyes as a challenge, usually leading to a fight. Do you? Who do you think you are now? Whom do you see reflected in the other's eyes?

Do this with a member of each sex. Do it in a mirror with yourself.

You Are What You See

In *The Fall of America*, Allen Ginsberg insists in the name of sanity that we disconnect our nervous systems from the media, which has, in essence and in literal fact, become a global nervous system. We have become nodes on its many branches and ganglia.

We are plugged into a diseased global nervous system through our eyes as we watch T.V., through our ears as we listen to radio, and through our fingers and eyes as we use computers or "surf the net." The global nervous system mediates or stands between us and immediate experience.

If you feel depressed, perhaps your electronic intake of depressing news is too high. Anxious? Too many anxiety-inducing commercials and harangues. Low self-esteem? Definitely too many artificial role models being processed by your already overburdened nervous system, which was basically designed by evolution for other things than information overload. Things like love, smelling flowers, and daydreaming.

Unplug once in a while or for good. Try not watching T.V., listening to radio, or reading anything for a week. Jot down your emotional state before you do this. At the end of the week of nervous-system autonomy, again note your limbic weather. Compare. The media has been telling you who you think you are. Who are you really?

A razor: Start today by not consuming any mediated information at all. Stop reading this book right now. Become im-mediate immediately. Continue reading tomorrow.

Shut Up!

Try to listen to the other person without thinking about your response as they speak. Shut off the interior dialogue and preconceived beliefs about self and other. Just listen. Give them that much. Give yourself even more. You might actually learn something.

Attempt this for a minimum of five minutes with a sympathetic friend who's been informed of the exercise. Then switch roles.

Scream Like Hell!

Dr. Arthur Janov popularized this as "Primal Scream" therapy. Using it, you can relive "core" experiences and release their pain and dysfunction. *Who you think you are* is something worth screaming about. Put this book down and scream right now as loudly as you can.

Go in Circles

Do you sometimes feel as though you're going nowhere, that you're only going around in circles? The bad news is that you are. The good news is that this is a very different spiritual practice called "circumambulation."

In a lot of religious traditions, one walks in a circle around a sacred object or mountain keeping a mindful and prayerful atti-

 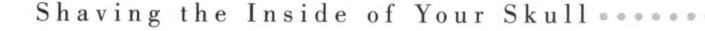

tude. Some do it for years, actually wearing deep paths in rock. You could try this for yourself around a large tree, statue, building, or even a chair in your kitchen. Do it a few times slowly, putting down beliefs about getting anywhere in particular rather than getting it together in general. Very restful, as well. Be where you are. And then be there again. And again.

Go in a Straight Line

Kinhin is the Japanese word for walking meditation. It's as highly valued as zazen or sitting meditation in Zen Buddhism. Just walk extremely slowly, almost a sort of Tai Chi walking; slow, even exaggerated motions. Be mindful. Pay attention. Mentally name each body part as they move with your walking: "Heel. Toes. Calves. Thighs. Pelvis. Chest. Arms. Hands. Head."

Try not to think too much, at least in terms of naming other things or labelling them good or bad. Notice the subtle gradations and changes of shadows. Nearly imperceptible temperature shifts as you walk. Shifting textures beneath your feet. Reality becomes nearly painfully delicate and exquisite as you savor it with this experience. Do this for at least ten minutes. Doing this razor will shift who you think you are in your head into who you really are: your moving body.

Don't Go

This is an exercise devised by Gurdjieff for his students. At random points during the day, Freeze! like in the kid's game. Do not move at all, even if you're balancing on tiptoe with a hot coffee in your mitt. Play statue. Look at this tableau you're part of.

Examine your posture and grace (or lack thereof). This is a snapshot of your normal unconscious interaction with life. Not a pretty picture. Or is it? That snapshot look at yourself will stand out in sharp contrast to the rest of the blurry and unfocused movie we usually and poorly act our way through.

Freeze right now for one minute. Resume reading.

Go Slow

Go slow-motion for a couple of minutes during a normal activity like drinking coffee, observing your movements and thoughts. The idea is sort of like in those slo-mo sports re-plays. The world generally slows down as well, so who's really running the show here? Pretend you're doing this underwater for a change of pace. Come up for air.

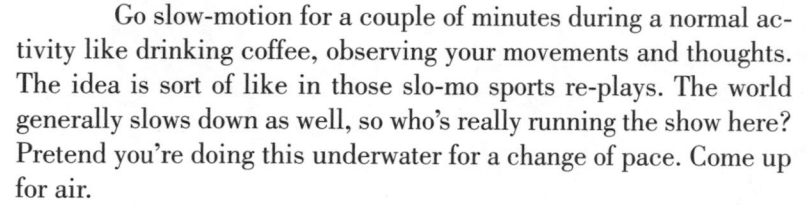

Go in Reverse

Try doing everything backwards for a few moments, as though the movie of your life were running in reverse thanks to an insane projectionist. You already feel this to be true sometimes, anyway. Sorry, you won't get any younger and won't be unable to undo mistakes and correct regrets with this one, but you will gain a unique perspective if you don't injure yourself.

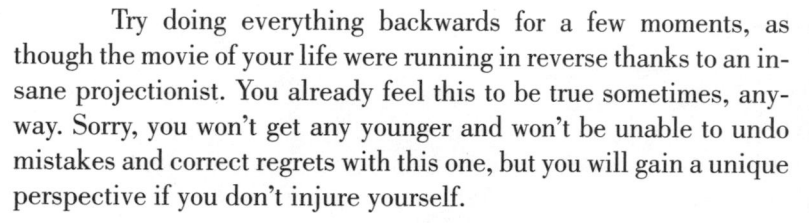

Go. Go. Go.

Mantra technique can be utilized as a means of do-it-yourself brain surgery. Pick a word that is charged with meaning for you, dripping with emotional content or even one that offends you.

Repeat it over and over for five, ten, fifteen minutes, however long it takes. Pretty soon, it'll entirely lose its "meaning" and just be an odd sound. You'll be surprised at how new and strange it sounds. Freedom from the words that describe our realities and form our beliefs, imprisoning us. Using those very words to free us from our cerebral cells. Try this both silently and aloud.

Map Your Body

Lie down on a piece of paper larger than your body. Spread-eagle and have someone trace your outline. Pretend this outline is a planet, odd-shaped as it is. Draw in imaginary continents, oceans, lakes, and islands. Label them. Perhaps your heart area is the "Sea

of Discontentment," your brain
island-continent called "Limitatia,"
fingers a mountain range named
"Seeker Mountains."
This is
personalized
the simul-
familiar
unknown,
think you
bravely
Lewis and Clark of
you can't get a big
just draw a body outline of
instructions. Another alternative is
draw and label body maps of each

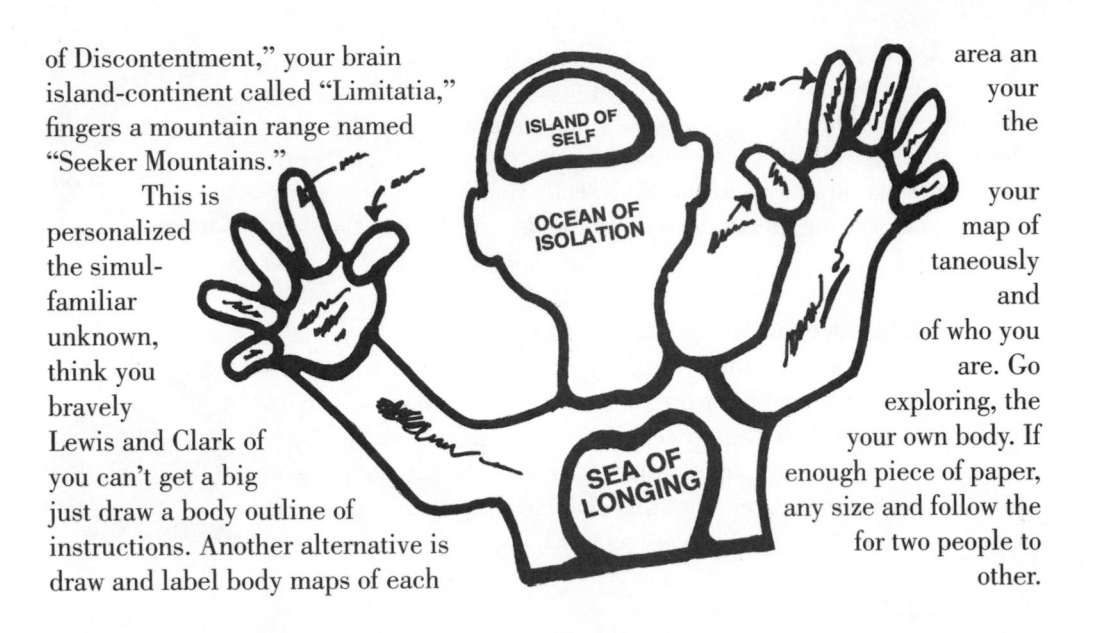

area an
your
the

your
map of
taneously
and
of who you
are. Go
exploring, the
your own body. If
enough piece of paper,
any size and follow the
for two people to
other.

Lose Control of Your Body

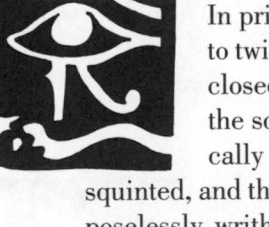

These are the instructions for a Subud exercise prescribed by poet Michael McClure in *Scratching the Beat Surface:*

In privacy allow the muscles of the body to do anything they please, to twist and turn as a baby does on a rug in the sunlight. The eyes are closed and the vocal apparatus begins to respond to the pleasure of the societally negated postures of the body (as one groans automatically under the hands of a masseur). The eyes are closed or squinted, and there is little or no visual stimulation. At first it is difficult to purposelessly writhe, twist, groan, cry, sing, chant, kick, twist, moan, weep, or laugh. Eventually, and after practice, after a number of trials, a mindless biological state is found. It then becomes easier to find the state, and one may exercise there longer and longer. If one develops this capacity up to thirty minutes or an hour, he finds on reclaiming his social person that he is in a euphoric state—a high. The senses see the brightness and auras and colors of objects around them and there is a feeling of physiological well-being. The experimenter will have been in a place where he, or she, was flying no banners but was a mammal—the universe experiencing itself.

Disable Your Body

Spend a day in a wheelchair.

Spend an hour blindfolded in your own home, sightless.

SHUT UP!!! Don't speak for an hour, day, or week. Use a chalkboard to communicate.

You'll soon see how controlled we are by the brain secretions and programmed beliefs we laughingly call "thoughts." The Japanese say it is easier to cut off your head than to shut your mouth. A good practice for keeping your head is to keep silence for part of the day.

Our real handicap is who we think we are. Adopting a temporary disability reveals a lot about our seemingly permanent self-images.

Relax Your Body

I have a habit of "scrunching up" my shoulders whenever I'm insecure, apprehensive, or just plain anxious. I became aware of this by paying attention to my own body language. I found that by consciously relaxing my shoulders, I could also release a lot of cleansing and positive energy as well: physical and emotional energy that I was foolishly storing in my muscles as a belief in my own inferiority or fear. Relaxing my muscles also relaxed the fear (belief) muscles.

Such a simple thing! Examine yourself for habitual physical defenses that impede a full and mindful life. Other places we store muscular fear are in clenched jaws, tight backs, and tense eyes. If you're brave enough, you might ask people close to you to point these behaviors out. Write down one place you store fear as tension.

Use Your Body to Relax Others

Speaking of body language, while you're at it, examine the body language of people in your life as well. A lot of learning how to read it is simple common sense. Watch how people armor themselves against you by folding their arms or crossing their legs, or how they open as well.

Respond to this language with your own non-robotic and conscious responses, seeing if you can't change whatever is happening by manipulating your limbs and evoking a change in the other.

Example: If someone has their arms and legs crossed while talking to you, resist the urge to do the same and keep your limbs open and receptive. Our verbal conversations are often a script we act out repeatedly and of little meaning. Look to the body for signs and symbols of the deeper dialogue and the real self.

How to Read Your Body

In the Penal Colony is one of Franz Kafka's most famous stories. Prisoners in the penal colony are subjected to a machine which inscribes their bodies with the name of the law they've broken: i.e., a disobedient person would be inscribed with "Honor Thy Superiors." The operation is extremely painful and, of course, fatal, as the "law" or commandment is actually cut into the flesh over the entire body while the prisoner is strapped into the diabolical apparatus.

A more contemporary writer, Clive Barker, sets up a similar image in his short story, "The Book of Blood." The protagonist in the story is also inscribed, this time with the stories told by hundreds of the dead who use his flesh as their means of communication with the world of the living. Their stories become minute traceries of scars covering his entire body. Says Barker, "Everybody is a book of blood . . ."

> Why do people
> Lavish decoration
> On this set of bones
> Destined to disappear
> Without a trace?
>
> —Zen Master Ikkyu

The razors, literal and poetic: Examine your own flesh and read it as your own personal book of blood, as the end product of a penal colony machine. What stories have been inscribed in your flesh as the result of the beliefs of others? What beliefs have you chosen to scar your own flesh with? It's only fair that I go first and perhaps give you an idea of what we're looking for here.

Me: I have a scar on my upper forehead as the result of a drunken fall years ago, the result of a personal belief in my own worthlessness and the belief that oblivion would "save" me from myself.

I am circumcised as evidence of the religious beliefs of my parents and the dominant culture at the time of my birth. On my left forearm is a scar the size of a quarter, voluntarily received as the result of a ritual burning when I took Zen Buddhist precepts to become a teacher.

Like many men my age or younger, my left ear is pierced. On my left arm is tattooed the Chinese character for "Happiness," on my right the Hebrew letters for "Life." (The piercings and tattoos were acquired during the editing of this book as a conscious experiment in exploring my own limits and beliefs about who I think I am.)

My hair and beard are long (my baldness more to do with genetics than fashion), signaling a cultural allegiance and belief system or maybe a self-exile from the mainstream. In Asia, long hair and beards were understood to be symbols of the renunciation of mainstream beliefs and values as much as Buddhist shaved heads.

You: Short hair or long? Shaved legs? Pierced ears? Cosmetic surgery? Tattoos (belief inscriptions par excellence, such as the classic "Born to Lose")? Colored contact lenses? Nipple rings? Hair dye?

The list is as long as the human need to terraform the planets of our "selves" into a shape that fits our beliefs about who we think we are. The "scars" and alterations can also provide clues as to just who our true self might be.

Are there also signs of other people's beliefs tattooed or scarred into you, signs that like Kafka's prisoner you have violated or adhered to some law by your very being? Concentration camp tattoo? Broken nose? Circumcision?

Examine yourself closely in the mirror after your next bath or shower. Can you read the language that you are? Make a list of every body alteration or adornment you can discover. Write the reason for it as well.

> If only we could pull out our brain and use only our eyes.
>
> —Pablo Picasso

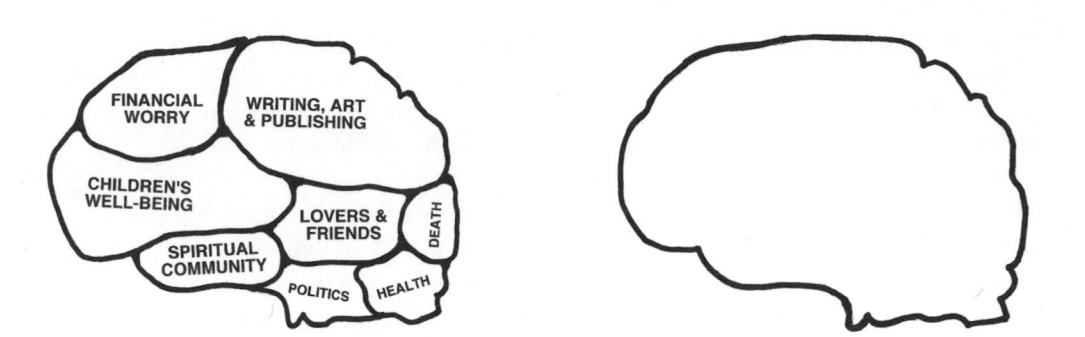

• • • • • Draw Your Brain

You don't have to actually remove your brain for this one and I'd strongly advise against it. Use the outline below this exercise if you don't know what your brain looks like (it, however, knows what *you* look like . . . it even has a mental picture of you it carries in its synaptic wallet. This is our chance to turn the mental tables!).

Allocate areas relative to size for the amount of your attention you spend on such things as sex, money, success, God, family, death, addiction, love, regrets, hopes, dreams, joy: you know these things better than I do. Outline them on your brain map much like continents or exotic countries. Who are the superpowers? Who are the undeveloped countries? Who needs aid or a revolution? Is there a mad dictator somewhere on this map?

We have maps to places we want to go. This is your map of where you're at and who you think you are. Update it frequently and as honestly as you can. Some of the techniques in this chapter are excellent erasers for the map.

Read with Someone Else's Brain

For years, I thought I was the only one in the world who did this one until I ran across this statement from Beat poet Allen Ginsberg about his relationship with poet and City Lights Book publisher Lawrence Ferlinghetti:

I always have him in mind as I write as I have a lot of people . . . I'm very conscious of what he would like and what he wouldn't like. Of his mind and abilities. It's not that they're the audience, it's that you look through their eyes. They're you. You become them . . .

One reads through someone else's brain. It's a very good trick and all poets should know it and most don't. It's psychedelic. You expand your own intelligence by including others. It's not hard to do. Like the guru leaves an imprint on your mind. They say even when the guru dies, his mind becomes the world, or the sky. It's because you have so much internalized his intelligence and his reactions by the imprinting of it. Like you've internalized your mother's and your father's. It's just part of your nature finally.

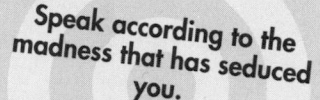

Speak according to the madness that has seduced you.

—André Breton

I often read and write through someone else's mind, literally taking on their personality as best I can. Not only do I receive the information in a new and sometimes startling manner, but I also, for a time, can step outside of my own egocentric beliefs and conditioning and begin to experience what it feels like to be another, to be someone other than who I think I am.

You can also listen to music, watch films and T.V., participate in any activities using someone else's brain. Attempt this by listening to music you enjoy with your father's brain. Watch a cartoon with a child's brain. Read this book with my brain.

Go Fly a Brain

Listed on the following form are the various centers and areas of the brain representing personal inclinations and abilities. By marking yourself (be honest) from 0 to 100 in each area and connecting the resulting dots with four lines, you will end up with what's called a "brain kite," or a geometric approximation of the inclinations, genetics, programming, and beliefs that make you "you."

What shape is your kite? Can it fly? Or do you always crash-land with yours? Now you know why. Try drawing your "ideal" one as well. This is a fairly accurate peek inside your biocomputer, but, of course, it is your brain, once again, that is making the decisions about scoring itself and so on. How can one be sure?

It's interesting to ask another brain (friend, spouse) to draw your kite as they perceive it through their own programming. When they tell you to "go fly a kite," now you know which one they mean! It'll probably differ radically from your own idea of your kite.

If you and a partner both draw your own kites (after copying or tracing them from the book), place them on top of each other and hold them up to a light to see where they are the same or different. In a large group of people, there are invariably at least two with identical kites.

Before filling out your brain kite, take a look at mine in order to get the sense of how to do this razor.

Author's Kite

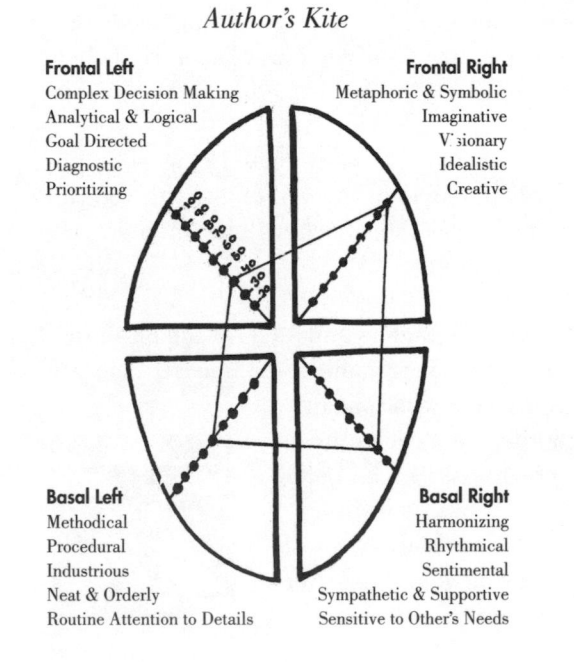

Frontal Left
Complex Decision Making
Analytical & Logical
Goal Directed
Diagnostic
Prioritizing

Frontal Right
Metaphoric & Symbolic
Imaginative
Visionary
Idealistic
Creative

Basal Left
Methodical
Procedural
Industrious
Neat & Orderly
Routine Attention to Details

Basal Right
Harmonizing
Rhythmical
Sentimental
Sympathetic & Supportive
Sensitive to Other's Needs

Reader's Kite

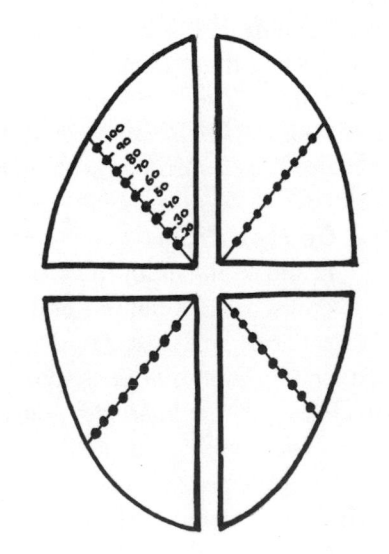

Brain Labels

Here are more diagrams of the stuff inside your skull that we are studying and attempting to shave, the central switchboard of perception and beliefs.

The following chart is of traditionally labelled diagrams of your brain, identifying the various centers. Study them for a while, acquainting yourself with the locations of your software (beliefs, imprinting, etc.) and understanding the terms. Then move on to the next razor.

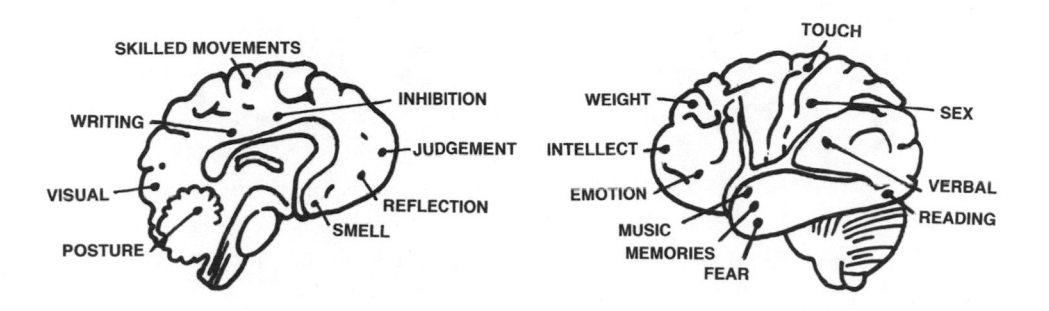

Brain Labels Brain

The next diagram contains the same graphics of the brain except I have removed the labels and shaved the inside of the skull for you. This was easier than you thought! Wow, was this book ever a good deal! Sorry, now you have to relabel your brain.

For example, where it previously said "Music Memories," write in your most memorable visual memory such as a car accident, concert, whatever. Where it said "Reflection," write in your most strikingly introspective moment. In the place of "Touch," the feeling you most like; for "Reading," the book that most influenced you. Where it says, "Sex," write in your most palpable fantasy or experience or taboo (or all of them). And so on with all the labels you can deal with. Some won't apply, although you can fudge some, like writing in your body image for "Weight."

When you're done, you'll have a nice little snapshot of the inside of your skull, you at your most "You-ness." This is what you're up against (or with). You could draw a new brain every day or week, reflecting on it for half an hour as a means to become who you really are. Meditating on your labels, perhaps you'll transcend them.

A word of caution: You will be using the very same brain to examine itself, so be suspect of the results. As Joe Friday used to say in *Dragnet:* "Just the facts, Ma'am," or to paraphrase Joe: "I carry a brain. I'm a human. It's my job."

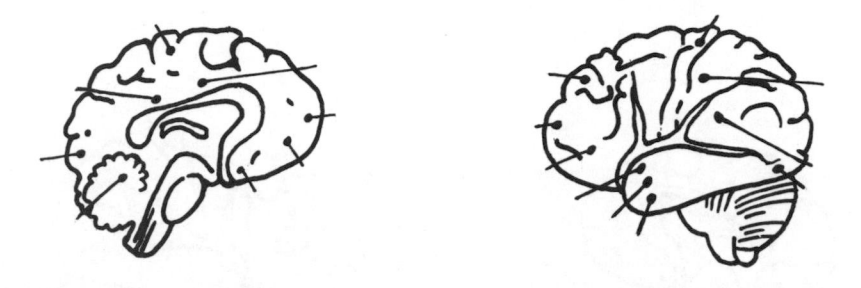

Remember: Part 1 is your brain. Part 2 is your brain on *Shaving the Inside of Your Skull.* Any questions?

Office Supplies for the Brain

When the thoughts in your brain are driving you crazy, you can use this technique to diminish their hold. Imagine that you have a tiny pad of Post-its inside your skull; you know, those little yellow pieces of paper with the glue on the back.

When you become aware of a thought about to think you into a pattern of belief and predictable behavior, write its name on a tiny imaginary Post-it, rip it off, and stick it to the thought as it goes through your skull.

For instance, if it's an angry thought, write "Angry" and so forth. By naming, identifying, and classifying our thoughts, as we did in the previous two razors, we gain power over them and lessen their hold over us. As soon as you label the thought, it sort of shrugs and moves along.

Our thoughts are the secretions the mind uses to digest experience, in much the same way that our stomachs secrete acids to digest food. Without our mindful attention to thoughts, they invariably seek out others of their ilk and band together in thought tribes or patterns called "beliefs."

These tribes of beliefs then colonize our consciousness and fiercely defend their territory, allowing little questioning or threats to their self-assured definitions of who we're supposed to be.

Label them. Stick little Post-its all over them until they quit. Freed of the belief tribes, you can think for yourself rather than being thought.

Are You a Problem Thinker? Brains Anonymous

This one was contributed by my friend, Providence writer and teacher Pam Steager. It is based on Alcoholics Anonymous' famous quiz to determine if you are a problem drinker (or alcoholic). She has simply changed "drinking" to "thinking" for our purposes below.

As we've seen throughout this book, the source of our suffering and limitations can be found in the frozen thought patterns we proudly call "beliefs." Transformation is possible for us, as sobriety is for the alcoholic, only in first admitting that we do indeed have a problem to begin with. So:

Are You a Problem Thinker?

To answer this question, ask yourself the following questions and answer them as honestly as possible, checking off each that you answer "Yes."

- ☐ Have you ever tried to quit thinking?
- ☐ Do you think first thing in the morning?
- ☐ Is thinking making your home life unhappy?
- ☐ Is thinking affecting your reputation?
- ☐ Do you think because you're shy with other people?
- ☐ Have you ever felt remorse after thinking?
- ☐ Have you gotten into financial difficulties as a result of thinking?
- ☐ Do you turn to lower companions and an inferior environment when thinking?

- Do you lose time from work due to thinking?
- Does your thinking make you careless of your family's welfare?
- Has your ambition decreased since thinking?
- Are you thinking right now?
- Do you think at a definite time daily?
- Does thinking cause you difficulty in sleeping?
- Has your efficiency decreased since thinking?
- Is thinking jeopardizing your job or business?
- Do you think to escape from worries or troubles?
- Do you think alone?
- Have you ever had a complete memory loss as the result of thinking?
- Do you resent the advice of others who try to get you to stop thinking?
- Do you think to build up your self-confidence?
- Have you ever been to a hospital or institution on account of your thinking?

• If you have answered yes to any one of the questions, there is a definite warning that you may be a problem thinker.
• If you answered yes to any two, the chances are that you are a problem thinker.
• If you answered yes to three or more, you are definitely a problem thinker and need to continue reading *Shaving the Inside of Your Skull*.

Only a person of great faith can afford to be a skeptic.

—Friedrich Nietzsche

Fourth SHAVE

Who We Might Become

Who we might become
is largely dependent
upon the beliefs that make up
who we think we are.

Who we might become
is an purposeful act of self-invention;
a conscious deconstruction of
who we're supposed to be
and who we're told to be;
a fearless act of disbelief
and a first step across the threshold
of our limitations.

Who we might become
is entirely up to us.

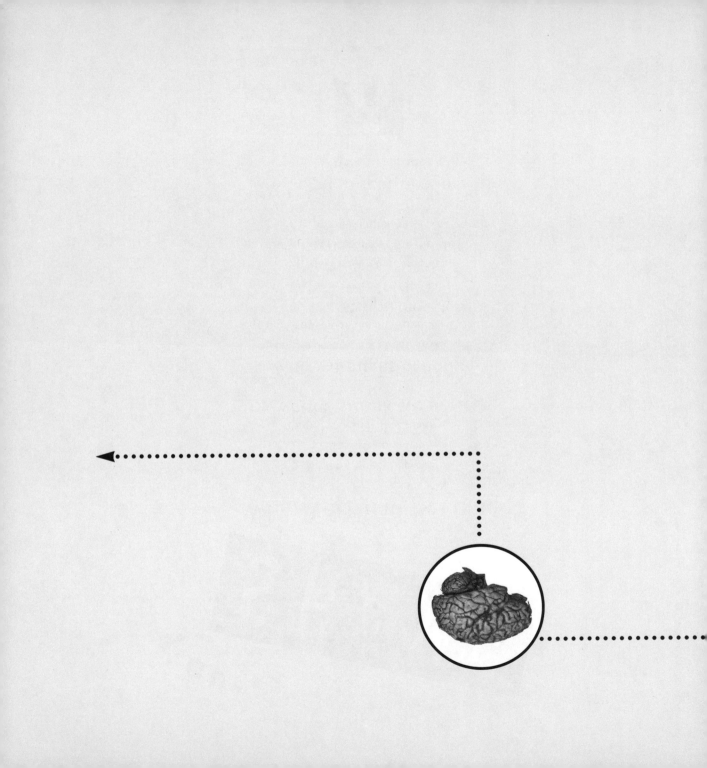

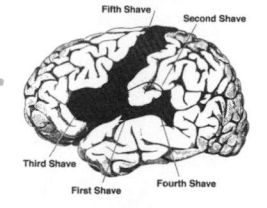

Fifth Shave
Second Shave
Third Shave
First Shave
Fourth Shave

BEYOND BELIEF:
DISBELIEF, UNBELIEF, AND BELIEF

We confront our lives with vast disbelief. If we are at all honest with ourselves, we know that we are amazed by the very fact of our existence. Thousands of years of philosophy, religion, myth-making, and war are the mute monuments to humanity's anxious attempt to make sense of existence. However much things change, the more this most basic of all instincts remains the same: a self-assured groping for the controls we desperately hope are real but are just out of our grasp. (Secretly, some of us fear that they might be all too real.)

Our quest for something to believe in is a mammalian whistling in the dark of the unfathomable graveyard of what we call the "known universe." Our instinct to believe, search for, and defend the objects of our belief even overrides our instinct for survival and self-preservation, sacrificing our selves for the gods and dreams that others have created for us and to which we give shape and substance with our longings for meanings.

Disbelief Is Wonder

To exist and be aware is to be conscious of our own sense of disbelief. Some systems call this anxiety, some dread, and still others the religious or spiritual impulse. By the time we reach our teens, most of us would laugh if told that our operative means of interacting with the world is disbelief.

More than a disbelief colored by the decadence of "mature" expectations, it is a disbelief shot through with goose-bump wonder and electrical possibility. We begin to *disbelieve* our previous opinions when confronted with something so marvelous, hideous, or outside our small storehouse of self that we have no intellectual or spiritual room to shelve or pigeonhole it. Our belief systems shut down and we are nearly one with the object of our attention.

How do we react to our place in this inter-action? Are we merely the audience? Are we insignificant in the grand scheme of "reality"? What is our place? Why are we alive? Why do we ask these endless, tormented questions? Are we really *who we think we are; who we're supposed to be?*

Profound disbelief pulls these questions from us like rotten teeth and we turn to the novocaine of religion, politics, or addictions for relief and self-assured spiritual numbness. For most of us, numbness is preferable to the very real pain we feel when put face-to-face with our lives and the inadequacy of our beliefs.

Our original state is one of perpetual and affirming disbelief. Most constructed belief systems are unnatural degradations of the human spirit and potential. A belief in a god or an ideology is, in itself, not necessarily a bad or even evil thing as mere tools or personal styles of spiritual approach.

It is when we confuse the tools with the job at hand that we become lost and diminished. It is when we worship the style over the goal and the form over the content that we die a little bit every day and with every thought.

Belief Is Lethal Fashion

Clever in devising and growing beliefs, we are stupid when we confuse them with the real thing. The symbols of a belief usually become more important than what they signify. Millions of people have died in the vain effort to prove the superiority of one symbol of belief over another. It is as ridiculous as arguing over which brand of jeans are the correct ones to wear. They both have the same purpose. They differ only in style.

So it is with beliefs. Believe this or believe that; it really doesn't matter. What does matter is our forgetting that belief is merely a constructed

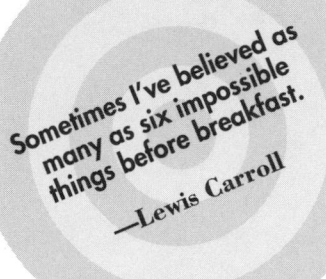

Sometimes I've believed as many as six impossible things before breakfast.

—Lewis Carroll

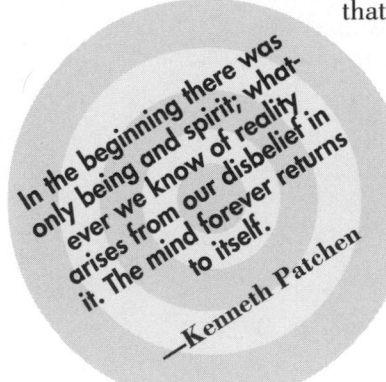

In the beginning there was only being and spirit; whatever we know of reality arises from our disbelief in it. The mind forever returns to itself.

—Kenneth Patchen

system of thought that attempts to make sense of the seemingly senseless. We are already dead and not truly living when in the grip of the beliefs that our ceaseless thinking churns out like plastic novelties to entrance and divert us.

Belief is like freezing a wave to capture its perfectly arched beauty. Belief freezes the world and our lives into static and dead snapshots, robbing us of the exhilarating ebb and flow of the current that beats in our veins.

Spiritual Nakedness

Spiritually, we are still in our infancy, frightening each other and ourselves with illusory differences in belief. Sometimes we even sacrifice the quality of our lives on the altar of belief. It is as much a matter of fashion as anything else. Our beliefs, ideally, can be the style in which we hit the target of personal meaning with the ball of our intent.

Spiritual nakedness and primordial disbelief mirror our original state and our original unsullied nature. Disbelief, in itself, is our original, unjudging, expansive, and reflecting mind. What have we been so afraid of?

Why then this great need for some sort of belief? If disbelief is so fundamental to our true natures, then why do we strive so hard to create artificial states of reality and pain for ourselves? Disbelief begets belief as night brings the day. Nature abhors a vacuum and seeks balance. For each, there is the other. For black, white; for male, female; for heaven, earth. Depend on this law only. You will obey it despite yourself. So it is with the dichotomy of belief and disbelief.

Unbelief Is Necessary for Belief

The existence of belief calls into being its opposite, a third dynamic in this trinity of consciousness: that of the process of *un*belief; that which belief seeks to oppose. Without opposition, the reason for belief's existence fades and disappears. The mind, essentially One, makes itself two in order to play this game of tension and fear when forced by its questioning nature to make sense out of the bewildering universe.

By making two rather than One, maybe things are easier to handle and the immensity doesn't overwhelm as much. The mind which is ours can

> Nobility begins when there is no longer any reason to have faith.
>
> —Kenneth Patchen

> All firm belief is a sickness.
>
> —Francis Picabia

choose one to believe in and the other to ignore. We become half-people living half-lives, believing ourselves satisfied with the answers yet actually fraught with fear and dread.

The belief in good and bad, form and emptiness, creates a belief in a god; a belief in self and life creates a simultaneous belief in non-self and death. That which originally motivated the creation of belief, that is, the fear of chaos and unease, becomes the cornerstone of belief. This is altogether different from the state of original disbelief which allows no opposites, acknowledges no qualities, good or bad, and sets up no tensions, except that of pregnant expectancy and creative uncertainty of the sort that takes your breath away in the face of overwhelming beauty and grace.

Disbelief = Nihilism?

Conventional, "normal" wisdom holds that the state of disbelief breeds all sorts of dysfunction, including fear, nihilism, selfishness, dread, and moral torpor. People can stand most any suffering and loss but the loss of their treasured beliefs. When this happens, they are left with only a "belief" in the solution of suicide and the essential meaninglessness of life.

Without beliefs, they feel, "I" cease to exist. This is *still* a belief, a desperate belief in meaninglessness and worthlessness. One actually *believes* one has no beliefs left. Belief is still alive and the invisible hand is still moving.

The very idea of meaninglessness is a human idea and an abstract creation. We, as a species, are terminally addicted to meaning and beliefs to explain every single thing under the sun. Stripped of the drug of belief, we go cold turkey and sometimes die, more often returning to pick up our insidious habit.

If we could admit our addiction and cease feeding it, the withdrawal horrors would soon cease and we would re-enter the world as it truly is, without the numbing and reality-altering effects of belief and "meaning." We would be awake rather than drugged and lulled into a complacent sleep, which we imagine to be reality. The opiate of beliefs substitute nightmare scenarios and fanciful dreams for the real thing.

Fear of Disbelief

We are afraid of our disbelief and justifiably so, because disbelief is the Void, the sunyata and emptiness of the Buddhist dharma; the death to self and cloud of unknowing of the Christian mystics, the undefinable omnipresence of the Divinity of Hasidism. All the great traditions counsel that we must die to our little ideas and beliefs of "What Is It?" in order to know "What It Is." A deliberate reclamation of our disbelief becomes a prerequisite to becoming *who we really are*.

Not cynical disbelief, mind you, but again that open and eager disbelief which constantly sheds limitations. This disbelief is anticipatory rather than explanatory; it is a mirror rather than a picture, and we can feel it as a perpetual motion toward freedom, not, like disbelief, as an anchor and imprisonment.

By believing something to be true, we, in fact, make it true, at least to ourselves. If we identify ourselves solely and wholly with our belief, we cease to exist in a universe of meaning when our beliefs are inevitably shattered. Wouldn't disbelief as a means of liberation only release the demons we've so carefully caged in what Timothy Leary calls our "neurological cages"?

I think not. By resting and centering ourselves in disbelief, we will have no need to seek elsewhere for assurance. We will have nothing to fearfully defend and nothing to lose. Or in the words of Lennon, "Nothing to kill or die for. No religion too." We can just Be. Lao-tzu repeatedly tells us that in order to lose something, we must have owned something.

Nothing to Depend Upon

You came into this life with nothing, least of all beliefs and expectations. You will leave this life with nothing but your beliefs about it. How much more secure to return to the original state of wonder and playful disbelief with which we were all born.

The Diamond Sutra says, "If the mind depends upon anything, it has no sure haven." Perhaps we can assume the opposite to be true as regards disbelief; that if the mind depends upon nothing, it *has* sure haven.

Disbelief is the instinctive compass with which we find our safe haven,

> Let sects multiply, till the time comes when every one of us is a sect, each individual.
>
> —Swami Vivekananda

> I think people are in love with the journey. People love seeking answers. If you were to suggest to people that the time of seeking is over and that the chore is now to face the answer, that's more of a challenge!
>
> —Terence McKenna

original meaning, or true selves. All forms of belief are broken compasses with which we lose our way while evading the central questions of our lives: What is this? Who are we really?

The regressive process of unbelief *unbelieves* the overwhelming facts before us and dissembles into rigid belief, separating the divine from the mundane, the sacred from the profane, and the magic from the ordinary. Unbelief, quite different from disbelief, refuses to confront anything beyond the realm of small belief and is the arm thrust out to stop that gift that disbelief bears us.

Reversing the Process

To awaken to *who we really are*, we must reverse the process, proceeding back along the scary, untamed road of self, unbelieving our previous beliefs and arriving where we began: filled with a wondrous and awe-struck disbelief that we are even alive and aware.

Disbelief is saving, ennobling, unchanging, empty, and capable of containing all things. Unbelief is destructive, inhibiting, and greedy in its need to devour wonder. Belief is the result of unbelieving. It is a paralysis of the spirit and the advance guard of death, just as disbelief is the herald of birth.

Belief systems are known for their extraordinary durability and their lack of self-obsolescent features. They are built for survival. They are not like your car or washing machine, self-destructing after a period of faithful service. They perpetuate and repair themselves, even as we writhe in pain from their irrational demands.

Abandoning Beliefs

The best and most honest of all possible belief systems would be one leading to its own abandonment after the goal has been attained. Buddha described this as leaving the raft of philosophy on the shore after having sailed it across the sea of questions. It would be ridiculous to haul it around on dry land. Something new is needed in these new conditions. Leave behind the raft of belief. Someone else might need it.

I think that the God whose face is turned to us is a God still struggling with the matter of Creation. He or She or It is still in the process of Creation, and we are feeling the imperfection of that process.

—Chaim Potok

The best way to conceive of the fundamental project of human reality is to say that man is the being whose project is to be God.

—Jean-Paul Sartre

Most beliefs fail this simple test, however, enslaving the believers to the heavy raft rather than helping them along their journey. Unfortunately, people seem to treasure the leaky and defective rafts most of all and are proud to shake the chains that bind them to it as they defend the freedom they say they have attained.

Breaking Out of Prison

Belief systems can be like prisons in which we imprison our free-flowing and untamed thought. Nietzsche viewed belief systems as windows:

". . . to look out this window, now out of that." It's only when we limit ourselves to one window that we become trapped by our funnelvision. The landscape of the soul demands that we smash the windows and even the walls.

Disbelief is the quality of innocent surprise like the feeling you get when a firecracker explodes. It's a surprise party thrown for you by your awareness.

Belief is the stodgy certainty which makes reality conform to its worst expectations. Unbelief is cynical and debilitating in its closure of frontiers and dreams.

Unbelief winks slyly and tells us that the real goal is elsewhere and obtainable at a price. Just fork over your disbelieving wonder, chum. It robs us of the truth we were born with and tosses it to the henchman of belief. We spend the rest of our days in a crazed race to retrieve it.

Disbelief Says, "WOW!"
Belief Says, "How?"

Use beliefs as tools. Appreciate them as art. But never confuse them with the real work at hand. Never be afraid to let them go when they've become obsolete or destructive. They're not life preservers on this sea of life. They're anchors, limiting us to one point of view and one range of experience. You will not drown without them. There is every possibility that you will instead soar straight up and looking down in disbelief say, "I never believed this was possible!"

Once you have moved beyond your beliefs, it is all, indeed, beyond be-

> My mind is my own church. All national institutions of churches . . . appear to me no other than human inventions, set up to terrify and enslave mankind, and monopolize power and profit.
>
> —Thomas Paine

> It is living and ceasing to live that are imaginary solutions. Existence is everywhere.
>
> —André Breton

lief. You will have moved to a form of disbelief which is also the road to *who you might become.* I believe I'll end here. Believe only that.

Who we might become
is an act of
spiritual transformation;
a transcendence of
who we think we are
to
who we really are.

But who are we really without beliefs?
Does disbelief equal
the death of meaning?

Who we might become
is by no means certain
until we have
at least examined
these questions . . .

The highest form of religion
is to transcend religion.
—Frederic Spiegelberg

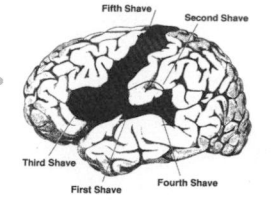

Fifth Shave
Second Shave
Third Shave
First Shave
Fourth Shave

THE MEANING OF LIFE

Zen masters often say that all other beings understand their correct jobs: dogs bark, clouds float, trees flower; only humans seem to have a neurotic need for something to believe in; something to justify their existence in terms of something greater, seeking the reason for every little thing.

The great need for a final, definitive answer to the question, "What is the meaning of life?" stems directly from our unwillingness or inability to accept our basic disbelief as our raison d'être, our job if you will. If our job is to simply be aware and attentive, full of awe and gratitude, then we're pretty poor employees and are in danger of losing our positions.

"What Is the Meaning of Life?"

This is the question that powers the engines of unbelieving and deadens our intuitive sense of disbelief and wonder. It is the padlock on experience rather than the key to our mortal cell. If we dare to ask the question in the first place, we must also be brave (or brazen) enough to then ask: "Why is there a meaning of life?"

In order to ask the question, "Is there a meaning?" we have to jump to "Why is there a meaning of life?" A vivid illustration of the futility of these sorts of questions can be found in this exchange between Alan Watts and Timothy Leary, taken from Leary's book *The Politics of Ecstasy.*

> Learning to savor the vertigo of doing without answers or making shift answers or making do with fragmentary ones opens up the pleasures of recognizing and playing with pattern, coherence within complexity, sharing within multiplicity.
> —Mary Catherine Bateson

Our Real Job

Leary asks Watts, "What is the purpose of human life?" Watts replies, "The purpose of human life is to ask the question: What is the purpose of human life?"

We could actually end this entire book right now so good is Watts's "explanation," but we'll push on like the good obsessive humans we are, working it to death and finding meaning in meaninglessness, and so forth, until we're all so bored and frustrated with these stupid questions that we all go get a cup of coffee or take a walk or do something *really* meaningful.

As Watts says, it is our *job* to ask these questions. Our real job is disbelief. Is it our job to answer them as well? Have we been trying to do somebody else's work as well as our own? Maybe this is why we're so confused and tired. Maybe we don't have the qualifications or even the responsibility to do this part. Maybe questions are enough.

Watts's reply points the way to a technique for a return to our natural state of awe and disbelief; to an actual method whereby we can even remove the itching need for Leary's question or any question at all. We can use the purpose of life as stated by Watts: ". . . to ask the question," to answer the question by exposing the fact that there's no need to even ask the question itself at all.

We Are the Meaning

Is there a meaning we can comprehend, even necessary for us to know? Can meaning lend anything to our lives that they don't already possess? In Dostoevsky, we find, "One must love life before loving its meaning." Albert Camus, reflecting upon this, comments, "When the love of life disappears, no meaning consoles us for it."

We are the meaning. Our meaning is our real job. We are only doing our job, which is to become ever more aware and conscious, even if it means inventing endless questions to fill our time and make the search more exciting.

All our beliefs and mad gropings for meaning and truth and answers to questions become mere metaphors. They have little significance in and of

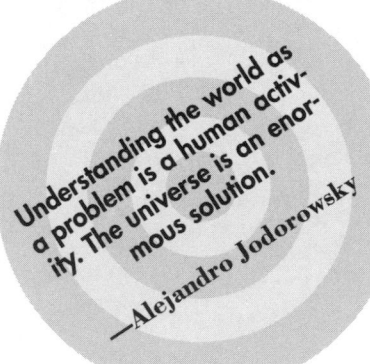

There are no solutions because there are no problems.

—Marcel Duchamp

Understanding the world as a problem is a human activity. The universe is an enormous solution.

—Alejandro Jodorowsky

themselves. They exist only as visible signs and proofs of something else, of something we desperately hope to be real and true. One person says *this* is the meaning of life, another says *that* is the meaning of life. Maybe I say *there is no meaning* of life. Who's right? Who's wrong? Who's to say?

Who Cares?

Who makes up these questions? Who is this "who" who is asking, anyway? Beat poet Lew Welch told this story: A tired student enters the philosophy professor's office, trembling and anxious. The student says, "I've got a question that's eating me alive. I've got to know! Sir, do I exist?" The professor snaps back, "Who wants to know?"

This is virtually the same exchange that can be found in this Zen tale: A Zen student asks the Zen master, "Who am I?" The Zen Master's answer? "Who's asking?"

Two tales, separated by thousands of miles and years. Two disciplines, separated by vastly differing techniques. Same question. Same answer: another question. Some unchanging truth is being exposed here. What is it? In asking, already answered.

Evasions and Excuses

It turns out that these questions about "meaning" and "purpose" are evasions and excuses. We invent them because we just can't bear to face the music of our disbelief. Zen masters and philosophy professors continually turn the questions back on the questioner. Our arrows of asking are bounced back by the reflective quality of our imagined target. There never has been a target, so why do we continue to fashion these torturous arrows from our quivering flesh and launch them with heartbreaking accuracy at ourselves?

Even when we take a direct hit and look up teary in our pain, we still refuse to admit that it was ourselves, *who we really are,* after all, that we were aiming for, not some abstract god, concrete belief, or clever script of meaning by which we hoped to act our way through our lives.

When we ask, "What is the meaning of life?" we are really asking ourselves to do our intended job: to question, to wonder, to stand in mute awe in the midst of this surprising universe.

> The secret is not to ask stupid questions.
>
> —Mr. Natural (R. Crumb)

> Tiger got to hunt, Bird got to fly; Man got to sit and wonder, "Why, why, why?" Tiger got to sleep, Bird got to land; Man got to tell himself he understand.
>
> —Kurt Vonnegut

When we dare to ask in the middle of the silent dark night, "*Is* there a meaning of life?" we are really asking ourselves to stop asking these circular questions and to rest content in the mind of constant disbelief; the mind that looks out upon all things as part of itself and has no need for self-justification.

When we finally ask, "*Why* is there a meaning of life?" we will only laugh aloud at our private joke that we're sharing with the world, the punchline being that we have *invented ourselves* with all these questions, all these endless desires, joys, and pains. The world is the raw stuff out of which we construct our beings and fates. Calcium for bones, protein for hair; questions for minds, love and loss for souls. Answers only for the womb and tomb.

> Live by the foma (harmless untruths) that make you brave and kind and healthy and happy.
>
> —Kurt Vonnegut

Questions

"Who am I?" "Who's asking?" The answer lies in the question. Can you feel it? Can you be brave, desperate, and alive enough to grab this question as your tool of liberation and set foot on the road to awakening and freedom? Or will you instead accept the normal beliefs offered you and choose to "live" out your time being "who you're supposed to be" and "who you're told to be"?

The real question is: Will you choose the drugs of belief and "ultimate meaning" over true unlimited, unconditional life and sink into a numbing, drowsy sleepwalk through this incredible landscape of being?

Spiritual Life Is Guilt

The impulse to attain answers that can be carved in rock or human flesh often stems from guilt; the guilt over abandoning our original state of disbelief and wonder. Rather than seeking a way back to the garden, the garden is subjected to a scorched earth policy of the soul. Thomas Merton had this to say about religions and spiritual questions:

> To base any religion upon a belief system is to invite rigidity and to risk an entrenched position.
>
> —Rae Beth

What I wear is pants. What I do is live. How I pray is breathe. Who said Zen? Wash out your mouth if you said Zen. If you see a meditation going by, shoot it. Who said "Love"? Love is in the movies. The spiritual life is something that people worry about when they are so busy with something else they think they ought to be spiritual. Spiritual life is guilt.

Carl Jung put it even more bluntly when he said, "Religion is a defense against the experience of God." Perhaps even the word and concept "God" is a defense against the real truth about ourselves and the realities we inhabit. Zen Buddhists say that if you see the Buddha in the road, kill him! Your beliefs and ideas about "Buddha" are standing in the way of your path to wholeness. So, too, with this "meaning of life" and spirituality business. If you can't yet bring yourself to kill these things, then try to excuse yourself politely and step around them.

So you see, what we call spiritual life is most often a sham and a quick fix for our insecurities. It is a fancy, shiny name for something dark and demeaning. True life has no need to call itself "spiritual."

> If existence had a final purpose, it would have reached it.
>
> —Nietzsche

Process, Not Product

We seek solidity in our answers about life. In so doing, we stand in its flowing stream, attempting to dam it with our arrogant wishes and expectations. The stream of life just flows right on around and past us. The answer is the *process of asking* rather than the *product of knowing*. It is in the passing and transient that we can experience the unchanging nature of life and thereby divine its true meaning.

The Crowfoot tribe said that life is the flash of a firefly in the night, the breath of a buffalo in the wintertime, the little shadow which runs across the grass and loses itself in the sunset. *The Diamond Sutra* cautions that this world is a star at dawn, a bubble in a stream, and a flash of lightning in a summer cloud.

Isn't this enough? Who could ask for more? To see things calls for our full and mindful attention, our childlike disbelief, not our ceaseless searching under rocks and skin for a meaning and purpose that exists elsewhere.

> There ain't no answer. There ain't gonna be any answer. There never has been an answer. There's the answer.
>
> —Gertrude Stein

For me, the words of my friend Reverend Tom Ahlburn of Providence's First Unitarian Universalist Church will have to suffice: "Things are the way they are because things are the way they are. That would be my guess. What's yours?"

The Questions

What is the meaning of life?
Is there a meaning of life?
Why is there a meaning of life?
Here at last are

The Answers:

Who's asking?
Who wants to know?

Fourth Set of RAZORS

Who we might become
is often the subject of speculation in
religion, art, and literature.
Who we really are
can be approached through some of their methods.

Confronting ideas about
death, God, and the meaning of life
can propel you beyond belief to
who you really are.
So can games and music.

Use this fourth set of razors to see
who we might become.

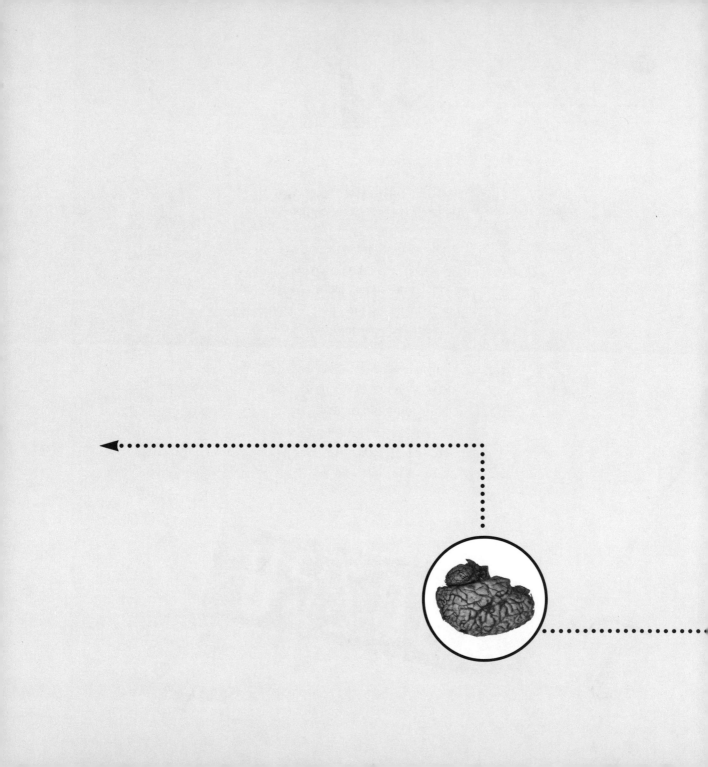

Something to Not Believe In

John Lennon's song "God" lists things he no longer believes
in. Limits, really. He sings, "I don't believe in magic, I-Ching, Bible,
Tarot, Hitler, Jesus, Kennedy, Buddha, Mantra, Gita, Yoga, Kings,
Elvis, Zimmerman, Beatles . . . I just believe in me, Yoko and me,
and that's reality." He even names the Beatles as a belief that limited
him.

Make up your own list of your own personal beliefs like
these to deny and shrug off. Start your list like this: "I don't believe in _____" and
then repeat for each belief, starting with the statement "I don't believe in . . ."

Try to list at least fifteen like Lennon did, particularly the really intimate and
self-defining ones (Beatles for Lennon). You can end your list, if you like, as Lennon
does, with a simple bare-bones belief that is not an abstraction like the others, a belief
in who you might become, for instance.

What You Don't Know Won't Hurt You and
May Even Possibly Help!

"You say, 'Why?' and I say, 'I don't know!'" sang the Beatles
in "Hello, Goodbye," pointing a way out of our brain's belief prison.
We believe we always have to know about absolutely everything, including the "Meaning of Life," thereby causing ourselves infinite
pain and shrinking awe and wonder. Agnosia, says Michael McClure,
is "the idea of knowing through unknowing . . ."

Agnosia, or unknowing, is a common thread in most spiritual traditions. In Zen Buddhism, one is encouraged to use the mantra "Don't Know" and to maintain this attitude of open, disbelieving mind. In the Christian tradition, one encounters the great mystical book *The Cloud of Unknowing,* which also advocates this unknowing of our assumptions and beliefs. *We must forget what we believe we know is true in order to really know.*

The Baal-Shem-Tov, founder of Hasidism, had these instructions, as told by Martin Buber: "The ultimate apprehension of knowing is that we cannot know. But there are two types of not knowing. The one is immediate: there one does not even begin to search and to 'know,' because it is indeed impossible to know.

"But another man searches and seeks until he *knows* that one cannot know. And the difference between the two: to whom can they be compared? To two who wish to get to know the king (here read: God, truth, etc.).

"The one enters all the rooms of the king, he rejoices in the king's treasury and halls of splendor, and then learns that he cannot come to know the king.

"The other says to himself: Since it is not possible to come to know the king, we shall not enter at all but resign ourselves to not knowing."

What sort of treasure are we missing out on by our resignation and surrender? It's not enough for me to tell you you can't know. You must unknow this yourself. From now on, suspend belief and engage in active disbelief before the brain gets a chance to describe reality for you.

Razors: Make a list of what you do not know. Stop when you reach one hundred items and write "etc." Keep the categories large, like "I don't know biology; I don't know quantum physics, . . ." List ten a day until you reach one hundred. Update this list periodically as you enlarge and revel in your areas of unknowing.

Sculpture Diary

Get some clay from an art store. It's called Plasticene, and comes in pound packages, different colors. You've used this in elementary school, I'm sure. You'll re-

Art is making the strange familiar and the familiar strange.

—Paul Klee

member the smell immediately. It never, ever dries up! I've had mine for twelve years now.

Place it on a board or similar base in an area you use daily, such as a desk, kitchen counter, or bedside. Work it once a day, changing, altering its shape spontaneously, automatically reflecting your state of being. Even if it starts to look really cool and "arty," continue changing it, even slightly if pressed for time.

As well as reintroducing you to your tactile senses and being fun, it will reflect your beliefs and teach you not only to flow with time but to be an active and willing agent in its flow.

If you could film your clay diary daily, a couple of frames at a time, you'd sure have an interesting movie in a year's time as you watched the clay flow and change like water, much like our own faces, lives, and beliefs. The sculpture diary is an ever-changing meaning of life.

Create Something. Destroy It!

On an episode of *Northern Exposure*, people ridicule Holling's paint-by-number paintings and he vows to give up art. Chris, the resident DJ and all-around spiritual mechanic, gives Holling a talk about art and how we are consumed by the products of our endeavors rather than the processes that led us there.

In order to break Holling of his addiction to his beliefs about self and "product," he has him burn one of his favorite paintings in the furnace.

Destruction is always implicit in creation, death always an attendant at any birth. To free yourself of a belief in a product-driven life, spend some time creating a piece of writing or art or whatever it is that you can do.

Destroy it. While you watch it being consumed or broken, you will feel a deep sense of loss and regret. At the same time, however, you'll experience

> Destruction is creation.
> —Bakunin

a novel sense of exhilaration and giddy freedom. The products of our lives are the dead-end destinations of our journey. The process is the endless dance.

Bow to Your Microwave

Give little bows to inanimate objects after you use them: cars, couches, toasters, books, houses, computers, dishes, beds, etc. An attitude of gratitude. Animate the inanimate! Bows can be physical bookmarks in the pages of our lives. Everything is helping you, moment to moment. Even this book. Bow to it right now. It would bow back if it could.

Listen with Your Feet

Go outside for this razor. Take your shoes and socks off. Standing on the ground (not asphalt or linoleum!), remove your attention from the other senses that are constantly reinforcing your belief programming and attempt to literally "hear" the earth with the soles of your feet.

Begin to feel the slight vibrations of passing traffic or machinery, the movements of moles and worms. Now extend the range of your new "sense" and feel the almost imperceptible rotation of the earth on its axis as it spins from day to night.

Listen even harder now, hearing through your feet the wide orbit your planet is describing in its immense journey around the sun, shining always above you, central and pivotal figure in your drama.

Become a Zombie!

No, not really, but it
consider the lessons of voodoo.
spells really work, according to
they are intrinsically true but
that they are. Belief is the real
The mind, most of all, is

might be profitable for you to
What makes voodoo curses and
cultural anthropology, is not that
rather the belief of the cursed
voodoo and the real curse.
the factor that creates the limits

of reality. Are we zombies, anyway, believing the curses of limitation and diminished potential that have been placed upon us? Are we the walking dead?

The razor: Make a "reverse" voodoo doll of yourself of clay, cardboard, wood, or fabric, maybe fastening a head shot cut from a photo of yourself for the face. Put a spell of wellness and growth upon it. Believe in this spell completely.

Instead of sticking pins in areas to be cursed, massage them tenderly, kiss them gently. Place symbols of what you wish to attain in its arms, symbols of your freedom on its head, and symbols of love at its heart. Burn incense and candles in front of it as symbols of illumination. Handle it at least once a day. At the end of thirty days, throw it away. You are now under the spell of something you've feared all your life: your self. This is who you might become.

Exquisite Corpses

My sons taught me this one. It's a common kids' travel game. It can be done with two or more people. The first person draws a line of some sort and passes the pad and pencil to the next, who adds another, and so forth (or back and forth) until you have arrived at a completely collaborative work of art. Have no final object or representation in mind during the process. Let the group flow determine the direction of the process.

This resembles the surrealist game of "Exquisite Corpse," in which various artists would draw different parts of a character, folding the paper over and passing it along until it was completed and opened, revealing the collective unconscious of the group.

This can be done as well with writing, each person adding a sentence, or even a word, at a time to a short story, letter, or poem. What is arrived at will challenge and transform your beliefs about personal creativity and uniqueness. You become part of a larger organism, revealing some surprising, magical, sometimes terrifying and occasionally ridiculous things.

Ghost Story

This is an ancient parlor game that uses the same technology as above except for different purposes. It works best in a large group of people. Whisper a very short story or rumor to someone, instructing them to pass it along. By the time it passes through all the people present and returns to you, it will have been so embellished, changed, and distorted that you might not recognize it as the one you originated.

You can do this as well over a longer time span, say in an office, family, or school environment, letting the story weave its way around for a few days. This is often called politics. Or you could ask people to wait a day or hour or whatever before passing it along.

We describe and create reality primarily through our words, written and spoken. Are they so reliable and unchangeable? Are our beliefs merely the mutated whisperings of other unreliable filters before us? Try this exercise out for yourself at your next gathering and observe closely the dynamics of perception and the all-too-human need to alter it to fit with personal history and belief.

The Kung Fu of Good Deeds

On an episode of the T.V. show *Kung Fu,* the Master tells Grasshopper, his young student, that if someone does you a good deed, you are in turn obligated to do a good deed to ten others. These ten are then obligated to do ten good deeds apiece.

By implementing this simple geometric equation, good deeds soon flow over the world. Next time, someone does you a good deed, go and do ten more.

"If sound is meaningless, I'm all for it."

So said minimalist composer John Cage. In his composition "4'33," a performer stood silently on the stage. Listeners were forced to focus on the quality of the silence or the "non-musical" sounds they inevitably heard: traffic, coughs, rustles.

Compose your own symphonies: start by picking a time frame, say 5' (five minutes). Keeping silent and still, pay uncritical attention to everything you hear, making no difference between good and bad, pleasurable or not. Just listen as you would to a piece of music, even pretending that you're hearing a CD. Try this right now for a couple of minutes before reading any further.

Start to apply this technique in longer and longer stretches until your entire consciousness is filled with the music of life, meaningless to your brain's beliefs about the organization of sound, perhaps, yet full of reality.

Zen Blues

Blues musician Maynard Silva says to listen to ten Elmore James records in a row. He guarantees this will rearrange your head and shave the inside of your skull. Other music might work as well.

Maynard says deep personal recognition of suffering fuels both the blues and Zen. I, myself, sometimes actually meditate to Side C of "Electric Ladyland" by Jimi Hendrix or the long jazz pieces of Charles Lloyd or Pharaoh Sanders. Become one with whatever you listen and meditate to; it doesn't have to be just sitar, ocean waves, chimes, or "tasteful" New Age music. Bring your life to the music as well as your ears, and the music shall set you free.

Your aural razor: Set your CD player on repeat and listen to a song of your choosing ten times in a row.

Dance Like a Dervish

Dervish dancing is an ancient Sufi practice during which the participants whirl in a circle, arms outstretched, palms up, head slightly cocked to the side. In this way, the dancer becomes one with Allah, God, or whatever. The music of Nusrat Fateh ali Khan is particularly suited for this purpose and is widely available.

Try this for as long as you can, maintaining an open, clear, mindful state of attention. Or just dance for the hell of it at inappropriate times. Just dance, OK?

Give It Away

The Laotians have a saying: "The more you want to own, the more you will die." Likewise, Thoreau has said that you don't own things, they own *you*. The native people of Vancouver Island, the Nootka, have a tradition called "Tloo-qwah-nah." The Europeans call it "Potlatch" and outlawed it along with most other forms of indigenous spirituality. As you'll see, it ran completely counter to the acquisitive, consumerist, and conformist thrust of Western culture.

In a Tloo-qwah-nah, a family literally gives away all they own after having accumulated this stuff for just this occasion. In so doing, they gain great stature in the eyes of their community. Not to worry. The family is not left bereft. Other potlatches and gifts soon returned them to a satisfactory standard of living.

While you might not want to go to this extreme, try a small potlatch, anyway, giving away the things that are robbing you of life. With each possession gone, you will also feel a removal of a belief that you had invested, like a spirit, in that object: a belief that it would bring you status, intelligence, health, luck, beauty, fun, whatever. Next time somebody admires one of your possessions, say a piece of clothing or a book, give it to them.

Shuffle Your Mind

Michael McClure has come up with this cool exercise in consciousness called the "Personal Universe Deck" for his writing students. The complete and extensive instructions for this can be found in his *Lighting the Corners*. I'll just give a basic overview of the method and encourage you to look up his full instructions and explanations.

Make a card deck of fifty blank cards, say 3x5 index cards. McClure says to carefully choose a hundred words from your vocabulary, words that will represent your personal universe, past, present, and future. Also the hundred words should sound "good" together.

Eighty of them should be divided evenly between sight (my examples: Black, Clear . . .), sound (Thunder, Guitar . . .), taste (Curry, Salt, Blood . . .), touch (Sand,

> If God lived on Earth, people would break His windows.
>
> —Yiddish saying

Skin, Granite, Cold . . .), and smell (Pine, Sandlewood, Ozone, Sweat . . .); sixteen to each sense. Be creative and personal.

Then ten words of movement, like swim, walk, fly, etc. One or two words concerning the body, its parts, functions. The rest are names of heroes (Kerouac, Buddha, Elvis . . .), invented personal words, birds (Falcon . . .), plants, totems, symbols (Crucifix), favorite dinosaurs, personal obsessions, abstractions like God, belief, etc., whatever is meaningful in your Personal Universe. None of any of the hundred words should have endings such as "-ing."

Says McClure about all of this, "Stay away from troublesome speculations. Forget philosophy and forget poetry. Give yourself over to the rules (of creating the deck). They're simple if you don't confuse them. It's about you."

Now write the words at the end of the cards, one at each end, like the Kings in a deck of cards. Shuffling them and picking three out at random, you will suddenly see the words and beliefs that you arranged in a new way.

Says McClure in conclusion, "There are lots of things to do with the cards: play games with them, make conversations with them, tell jokes with them, make sound poems with them . . ."

A random card deck poem from me: "Swim Black Buddha!, Green Brain Moan!, Stroke Skin Moss." Here's what one should look like:

Right Now!

This is something that I attempt to do regularly. At random points during my day, I say to myself, silently or aloud, depending upon social (or antisocial) circumstances, "RIGHT NOW!!!!" What is the purpose of this?

Well, first of all, it feels like a strong hit of caffeine in my spiritual system. What it does is to, in a very real and demonstrable way, literally center you in this moment and space, no longer delaying your life. For that instant, you *are* as you *are*, which is really all that this is about. Said Rabbi Hillel, "If not now, then when? If not here, then where?"

Don't wait a second or year longer or until you have the time, money, serenity, knowledge, meet the right people, teacher, etc. (you already know all the excuses!). Right now is your time! Always is. Always has been. What are you waiting for? Why are you still reading this and looking for an answer? This is the most serious and essential method in all of *Skull,* so put the book down (right now) and say aloud, with conviction: RIGHT NOW!

Right Now Again!

Ram Dass presents these methods in *Be Here Now.* Here is his exercise right now:

> Set alarm clocks or design your day or put up notes on the wall so that a number of times during the day when you are in the midst of various occupations you confront yourself with the questions:
> (a) Where am I? and then answer: Here.
> (b) What time is it? and then answer: Now.

Each time you do this, try to feel the immediacy of the Here and Now. Begin to notice that wherever you go and whatever time it is by the clock . . . it is always HERE and NOW. In fact, you will begin to see that you can't get away from the HERE and NOW.

Start Your Own Religion!

This is the advice from Timothy Leary in *The Politics of Ecstasy*. He says that in order to make your religion work you should "write down and define your: Goals, Roles, Rituals, Rules, Vocabulary, Values, Space-time Locales, Mythic Context. Develop your own rituals and costumes . . . You will eventually find yourself engaged in a series of sacred moments which feel right to you . . . Unless you form your own religion and devote an increasing amount of your energies to it, you are a robot. Your new religion can be formed only by you. Do not wait for a messiah. Do it yourself. Now."

Your razor: What would be the name of your personal religion? What would be its major belief?

Criticize Other Religions

In William Blake's "Marriage of Heaven and Hell," we find the following spiritual autopsy report and attempt at reanimation:

> All Bibles or sacred codes have been the causes of the following errors:
> 1. That Man has two real existing principles: Viz: a Body and a Soul.
> 2. That Energy, call'd Evil, is alone from the Body; and that Reason, call'd Good, is alone from the Soul.
> 3. That God will torment Man in Eternity for following his Energies.
>
> But the following Contraries to these are True:
>
> 1. Man has no Body distinct from his Soul; for that call'd Body is a portion of Soul discern'd by the five Senses, the chief inlets of Soul in this age.
> 2. Energy is the only life, and is from the Body; and Reason is the bound or outward circumference of Energy.
> 3. Energy is Eternal Delight.

Three razors: Try to construct your own list of three commonly accepted and sequentially dependent beliefs. Refute them as simply as Blake did. Delight in them.

• • • • Losing My "Religion"

Write down at least six qualities that come to mind when you think of the most "religious" person you know. Most people, when asked to do this, will write down qualities such as "goes to church regularly" and "believes in God." Are those "religious" qualities or are they actually indicators of rigid beliefs of both parties, described and describing?

The person I consider the most deeply "religious" person I know is a loudly and proudly self-proclaimed atheist who is active in his later years in issues of social justice, ecology, and equality. He pretends outrage and insult whenever I describe him as "religious," but he knows what I mean. Atheist that he is, he refuses to believe it!

So what would you consider to be the six "religious" or spiritual qualities of a person close to you? This might surprise you as it shows more about our own beliefs than those of the person we're attempting to describe.

See God

See divinity in every being and thing you encounter today. Literally. Make the conscious effort to do this in a very real way. Treat them as you would God.

After a couple of hours of this, you'll be feeling very blissed out, almost high. It's scary, but it's the way people like Ramakrishna, Jesus, and Buddha apparently felt all the time: God-intoxicated. Do this especially if you don't believe in God. It still works! Try this for at least a half hour today, pretending that God's hiding in everyone and everything, playing hide-and-seek.

Don't See God

The Hindus call this meditation practice "Neti, Neti" or "Not here, not here," meaning God isn't here. Spend ten minutes pointing at things, saying to yourself, "Not here" as you don't look for God or ultimate meaning. Do it during the day if you get too obsessed with something. Say to yourself, "Not here. Not this."

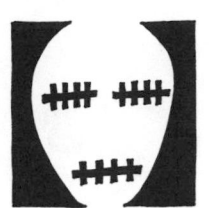

A razor: Point at this book and say, "Neti, neti." Point at your heart and say, "Here, here."

How to Find Your Lost Day

Carlos Castaneda's Yaqui teacher Don Juan taught him an exercise called recapitulation. I'd read about it long ago but had forgotten it until a middle-aged cab driver named Ray was giving me a ride from the airport in Providence and, in making small talk, asked what I did.

I told him also about writing this very book you're now reading. He got excited about the topic, asking me if I'd ever tried Don Juan's recapitulation. I was beginning to feel like a naive Castaneda myself as this unlikely and unexpected cab driver and teacher explained it to me.

At the end of your day, place your chin on your right shoulder. Slowly swing it until it's resting on your left shoulder. As you do this, review the significant events of your day in chronological order. In doing this, you will expose significant patterns, perhaps foresee further developments, and confront your belief systems in a conscious effort to transcend them and see who you might become. Do this recapitulation exercise before you sleep tonight.

Two lessons here: the first, obviously, from Don Juan, the second from cabbie Ray: your teachers are everywhere, just waiting for your consent to teach you. Assume nothing about anyone except to assume that everyone is a Zen master in disguise.

> The secret of a warrior is that he believes without believing . . . To just believe would exonerate him from examining his situation. A warrior, whenever he has to involve himself with believing, does it as a choice.
>
> —Don Juan
> (Carlos Castaneda)

How to Find Your Lost Keys and Life

This is another teaching I received under circumstances similar to the preceding story. When I lived in western Iowa, I became friends with an elderly plumber named Pat, a rough-and-tumble-looking guy who was descended in part from Chief Keokuk.

This is how we met: Pat was driving by my house one day as I was on my hands and knees in the grass, desperately looking for my lost car keys. He got out and without introducing himself told me that I was going about it all wrong. He said that most people can't find things because they focus obsessively only on a small point as they scan and search. Our beliefs limit our attention to a pinpoint rather than expanding it.

Instead, he said to unfocus my eyes and to look without really looking, sweeping the area, taking in the entire field of vision and not one individual spot after another. It also helped, he said, to remove the object from your mind, that is, not to think about finding it so intently.

I tried it. I found my keys almost at once and to this day I employ the same technique when searching for keys, fulfillment, love, or meaning. You can try it, too.

The razor: Unfocus. Clear your mind. Scan the room for a couple of minutes. What do you see through this non-specific seeing?

Death Is Your Best Friend

Gurdjieff said, "One of the best means for arousing the wish to work on yourself is to realize that you may die at any moment. But first you must learn how to keep it in mind." Don Juan said that Death is always looking over our left shoulder.

> You have nothing to do be-
> fore dying.
>
> —André Breton

Your razor: Pat your left shoulder lovingly and smile whenever you get lost in the details. Pat your left shoulder right now and say out loud, "I'm going to die someday" before you read any further.

Your Skeleton

This is a visualization by Vietnamese Zen Master Thich Nhat Hanh from *The Miracle of Mindfulness*.

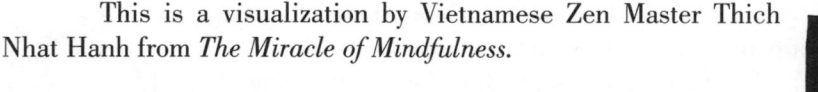

Lie on a bed or on a mat or on the grass in a position in which you are comfortable. Don't use a pillow. Begin to take hold of your breath. Imagine all that is left of your body is a white skeleton lying on the face of the earth. Maintain the half smile and continue to follow your breath. Imagine that all your flesh has decomposed and is gone, that your skeleton is now lying in the earth eighty years after burial. See clearly the bones of your head, back, your ribs, your hip bones, leg and arm bones, finger bones . . . See that the skeleton is not you: Your bodily form is not you. Be at one with life. Live eternally in the trees and grass, in other people, in the birds and beasts, in the ocean waves. Your skeleton is only part of you. You are present everywhere and in every moment. You are not only a bodily form, or even feelings, thoughts, actions, and knowledge.

> Man is the only animal that has the True Religion—several of them. He is the only animal that loves his neighbor as himself, and cuts his throat if his theology isn't straight.
>
> —**Mark Twain**

You might, like the tantric practitioners, try this one out in a graveyard at night, but then again, maybe not. A variant of this exercise is to lie still, visualizing the actual step-by-step decomposition of your body.

Your Corpse

Jack Kerouac recommended this procedure for whenever you're feeling sorry for yourself or full of self-importance. Whenever you're deep in it, go look in the mirror, point, and say sternly: "Who dragged this corpse here for you to look at?" Go do it right now. You're dying a little bit each time you read these words.

The Skull Speaks

Chuang Tzu, while traveling, saw an empty skull. He hit it with his horse whip and asked, "How did you come to be like this? Did you live a wild life and destroy your health? Were you executed as a condemned criminal? Did you shame your family and commit suicide? Did you die of starvation and thirst? Or did you live long and die of natural causes?"

The skull didn't answer, so Chuang Tzu used it for a pillow as he slept. The skull appeared to him at midnight in a dream and said, "What you asked about are the troubles of mortal life. When one dies, one doesn't have those troubles. Would you like to hear about life after death?"

Chuang Tzu said yes. The skull said, "In death, there are no kings, no subjects, no change of seasons. One is totally free, seeing heaven and earth as spring and fall."

Chuang Tzu didn't belive him and replied, "If I asked God to give you back your life, your bones, your flesh and skin and return you to your parents, family, and neighborhood, would you like that?"

The skull looked serious and said, "Why would I trade the happiness of a king for the countless troubles one meets in the world?"

Here we have an extreme example of shaving the inside of your skull.

The razor: Imagine yourself as a skull giving advice to a passerby, much like Chuang Tzu.

What on earth would you tell them? Would you take the second chance at life? Have you taken your first?

> You don't get to choose how you're going to die. Or when. You can only decide how you're going to live. Now.
>
> —Joan Baez

What Will You Say Before Their Funeral?

Visualize the death of the living person closest to you and go through the entire process in your mind and heart. Allow yourself to experience the grief and loss and regret in its entirety.

Return the person to life at the end of the exercise. There are now no tomorrows left in which to say "I love you" or "thank you" or "I'm sorry." Write down one regret you came up with. One fond memory as well. Share it with them.

What are you waiting for? This book will still be here.

What Will They Say at Your Funeral?

We've all, when in self-pitying moods, fantasized about this.

Your razor: Write a eulogy for yourself pretending you died today and that it'll be read at your funeral. Limit it to three paragraphs. Is this how you want to be remembered?

Your Last Words

What would your "famous" last words be as you die? Write them down and put them where you can see them for a week. Maybe limit them to no more than three sentences. Send them to friends and family.

After the Funeral

All our "stuff" and "things" will outlive and outlast us, so why do we cling so tightly to them as though they were a raft across this sea of mortality? This razor calls for you to go through your stuff as though you were already dead.

Why let your kids and relatives and (God forbid!) strangers have all the macabre fun? What would you keep out of all the flotsam and jetsam that is the leavings of your life? What would go in the yard sale, to the Salvation Army, to the archives, saved for ancestors?

Pretend your stuff is the stuff of a dead person. Examine it like an archaeologist for clues as to the life lived. Remember the life this person (you) lived as you handle this stuff lovingly and longingly. If you're brave enough, start giving some of this stuff away. I've had to do this for dead relatives a couple of times, going through their intimate possessions, sorting, prioritizing. It's unspeakably sad. Doing it alive is unbearably liberating.

Whenever I get psychologically crushed by all my "stuff," I just wave my hand in dismissal: "Oh, this stuff? It belongs to a dead man. Want some?"

What Kind of Funeral?

Tibetan Buddhist funerals are called sky-burials, similar in nature to the scaffold burials of the Plains Indians, in which the dead person was placed on a scaffold erected in the open air. In the Tibetan funeral, the body is placed in the mountains. Birds and wild animals do the job of disposing of the edible remains. In this way, the cast-off body is returned to the earth from which it sprang.

Think about your own funeral arrangements and what you would like them to say in a larger context. Cremation? Embalming? Donation to a medical school? Taxidermy? Make these arrangements ahead of time, if so inclined. How we die says a lot about how we will live.

How to Tell If You're Dead

You probably need this right about now after all the preceding talk about dying. The formula for determining if you're actually dead is from my friend Unitarian minister Tom Ahlburn and is always included in his sermon at Easter time:

Every year I ask this same set of questions of you—and of myself as well. I got them from Frederick Buechner, our neighbor in Vermont. I want to find out if you are resurrected this morning—if I am. Maybe you remember them. If so, I wonder if your answers have changed.

1) Have you wept at anything during the past year?

2) Has your heart beat faster at the sight of young love?

3) Have you thought seriously about the fact that some-day you are going to die?

4) More often than not, do you really listen when people are speaking to you instead of waiting your turn to speak?

5) Is there anybody you know in whose place, if one of you had to suffer great pain, you would volunteer yourself?

As the Zen Master was about to die, he stood on his head. His disciples were aghast and asked why. "Because it's never been done before," he said as he died and toppled over.

—Zen anecdote

If the answer to all or most of these questions is no, the chances are that you're already dead.

If you've determined that you're *not* dead, you'll be able to continue reading the Fifth Shave.

My life was a risk—and I took it!

—Robert Frost

Fifth SHAVE

Who We Really Are

Who are we really?
Who we're **supposed** to be, who we're **told** to be,
and who we **think** we are is submission,
limitation, and death.
It is belief.

Who we **might become** and
who we **really are** is fluid, unpredictable,
and **alive**.
It is disbelief.

Who we really are

can be found in the extent of our continual and fearless revolt
against beliefs and forces,
within and without,
that limit us with fear.

Who are we really?

We are as small as our farthest limits.
We are as large as our nearest revolt.

183

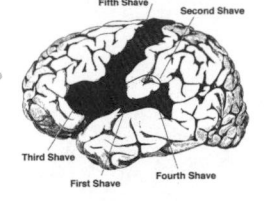

REVOLT!

You hear an awful lot of talk about "truth" and "reality" from the salesmen of beliefs. They want you to define yourself in terms of their particular "product" and brand yourself as "Buddhist," "Republican," "blue-collar," "victim," "addict." The list of personal labels is as endless as the pitch. The financial high priests, as well, dictate the current economic theology and which economic god is demanding our monetary worship.

Our own secret beliefs about our worth or worthlessness pull the strings of our puppetlike behaviors. What is common to all these approaches is the promise of some sort of fulfillment, of "security," of becoming "yourself."

It's a lot like those commercials on T.V. that come on between shows. The volume is twice normal as though they think they can shout us into purchasing their products or beliefs. All the while that they're yelling and blaring about how our lives are incomplete and would be much better with their item, the toll-free number for ordering flashes like a strobe light on the screen. I suppose they think that the sheer intensity of their visual and sonic attack will move us, zombielike, to the phone. We can scoff at this all we want to, you and I, because we can either turn it off or leave the room.

But how about the more insidious pitches with lulling and soothing tones that we are daily surrounded by and assaulted with? Are we falling, rubelike, for subtle promises of freedom that are just the same old crap repackaged in a more spiritually, economically, emotionally, or politically correct image? What is it that we are so susceptible to? What is the real goal of all this frenzied buying and consuming and defending of beliefs and labels?

Faking It

In short, it is the human need to know and understand one's self in the face of certain death and a seemingly indifferent universe. We all feel incomplete somewhere, bogus really, as though we were wearing masks and carrying charms to ward off the darkness of both the scarily unknown and the all too familiar and terrifying known. I think that most of us have a secret fear that one day "The Guy in Charge" is going to walk into the room, point at us, laughing, and say, "You're a fake!" We surely cast our gods and politics in this shape. We will go to any lengths to feel authentic, solid, and real.

At root, *all* attempts to make sense of human existence rest on this very primal insecurity and existential disease. They offer ways to stop being a "fake" and how to become "real." What is held out as the antidote is the attainment of one's "true self," whether defined in terms of one's place in an economic system, as in Marxism, as an obedient child of God in Christianity, or maybe as a loyal, unquestioning employee in an impersonal corporate structure. Most of us willingly lose ourselves and call it discovery. Most of us gladly accept slavery and call it freedom.

Something That Doesn't Change

Do we know ourselves at all? Have our beliefs about self been a constant? Look at a picture of you as a child, a teenager, and adult. What connects these three different individual beings? The beliefs we held as children are most likely totally gone by now, so who are we really? Our bodies, as well, have been altered beyond recognition by one of our earlier stages.

What has remained constant is our awareness and its attendant sense of disbelief, its uncritical attention to the here and now. The mind limited by beliefs continually changes, but the awareness of "self" is unchanging. It

If sex and creativity are often seen by dictators as subversive activities, it's because they lead to the knowledge that you own your own body (and with it your own voice), and that's the most revolutionary insight of all.
—Erica Jong

Just say know.
—Timothy Leary

is a continuum from there to here to where? It inhabits all the various sizes, shapes, and styles that you have ever been and will be.

Uncritical and unopinionated, this awareness has always been the accepting movie screen on which we've projected the multitude of dramas as growing and dying beings; it is like a clear glass that takes on the colors of the emotional or ideological fluids poured into it. Without this simple awareness and attention, all other beliefs, minds, and styles would have no impartial observer present in the form of memory and hence, no existence, much like the old "if a tree fell in the forest and there was no one there to hear it . . . ?"

This awareness is called many things by many systems, usually, as we have seen, to sell you their system, but it is universally acknowledged nonetheless as "true self," Buddha Nature, Original Mind, God, Wankan Tanka (The Great Mystery of the Lakota), living in the Body of Christ, self-realization, satori, enlightenment.

> Freedom is free of the need to be free.
>
> —George Clinton

Revolt Is Biological

How can we approach our true selves and become *who we really are* without polluting our potential with these descriptions or degrading it with systems and methods? How can we actually shave the insides of our skulls and break the bonds of belief and programming? Remember the slogan that so impressed Theodore Parker as a child? "REBELLION TO TYRANTS IS OBEDIENCE TO GOD."

Michael McClure writes that *revolt* is part and parcel of our biological fail-safe, that revolt is the means by which we can attain freedom. He continually refers back to the wisdom that is stored in our very meat. The Surrealists, as well, called for a state of *perpetual revolt* as a style of being.

Revolt against exterior forms of belief-mongering is easy and ultimately futile in this work of awakening. It is against *ourselves* that we must revolt, and this is the hardest and most dangerous form of subversion of all. We set traps for ourselves constantly, booby-trap our spirits, and hide snipers in our brains.

> Every so often, I revolt, even against what I believe with all my heart. I have to attack everything, myself included. Why? To simplify things. We know too much—and too little.
>
> —Henry Miller

We are so well programmed to expect failure, disappointment, and rage that any attempt, even on our own behalf, to revolt against this mess is met with swift and reactionary force, usually in the form of stress, neurosis, or compulsions. Transcending these mean-spirited defenses, we can reclaim our own lost territories.

Revolt Is Spiritual

Said Buddha, "A man conquers a thousand men. Another conquers himself. I consider the latter the greater." Says McClure, "At all times revolt is the search for health and naturality . . . All revolt is personal and is against interior attitudes and images or against exterior bindings of Society that constrict and cause pain."

Any effort whatsoever made to attain your true unconditional self will be seen as a threatening revolt by both your own limiting belief systems and by your cultural context. The resistance within and without will be incredible. There will be pain. By these signs, you can know that your path is correct and awakening nearby.

Rebellion and revolt against our acquiescence in sleep and limitations are the discernible movements of our true self. Our gnawing guilt, fears, and dread all spring from our reluctance to do our real jobs of spiritual rebellion: rocking the boat and learning to swim for ourselves in the sea of life. How do we choose our points of rebellion against the things that enslave and lessen us; where do we take our stands? In the 1950s biker movie *The Wild Ones*, a "square" character asks Marlon Brando what he's rebelling against. Responds Brando, "What've you got?"

The War Against the Imagination

Hypnosis, sleep, slavery, programming, and a living death are falling from you like dead leaves as you seek transformative experiences, revolt, and shave the inside of your skull. Poet Diane diPrima said that "the only war that matters is the war against the imagination!" Your imagination is most often your only weapon in this battle to know yourself, usually the best razor available for shaving the inside of your skull. Use it freely and uninhibitedly as you revolt and become who you really are. Imagination makes you truly human, unique, and less pliable.

No wonder a war is being waged against imagination on all fronts from the time we can begin to think. We are instead encouraged to think other people's thoughts, live other people's fantasies, and die other people's deaths. Our schools, entertainment industry, religions, and governments all have taken up arms of guilt and force in their war against your imagination. Revolt! Imagine instead that you are whole and free. Unplug the biocomputer of your mind from the endless stream of cerebral confections and spiritual carcinogens.

> You wait for fate to bring about the changes in life which you should be bringing about by yourself.
>
> —Douglas Coupland

The Great Refusal

Herbert Marcuse called this process "The Great Refusal." Refuse to sleep your life away. Refuse to consume the drug of limiting belief and substitutes for real experience. Refuse your false self and reclaim your own integrity. In your sleep, dream that you are waking up.

Revolt against that which is the most revolting indeed: our degradation, consumption, and complicity in the violence, rage, and lack of love in which we wallow and consider our home. Resignation and a sense of powerlessness is the goal of all programming and limiting beliefs. Shrug off instead your chains. If you find it all revolting enough, regurgitate the stuff you've been swallowing about yourself. Revolt!

> In some instances it is a custom, a venerated tradition, that is fundamentally immoral. We cast them overboard and raise the cry, "Down with morality!" It becomes a duty to act "immorally." A higher morality has begun to be wrung out.
>
> —Peter Kropotkin

 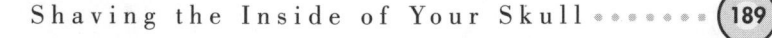

Personal Revolution

Emerson describes the condition of the person attaining freedom through revolt: "He who knows that power is inborn, that he is weak because he has looked for good out of him and elsewhere, and, so perceiving, throws himself unhesitatingly on his thought, instantly rights himself, stands in the erect position, commands his limbs, works miracles; just as a man who stands on his feet is stronger than a man who stands on his head."

What will be left after our personal revolution? Will we erect new and shinier prisons and citadels of belief for ourselves? What, after all, is this true self we keep referring to? All I know for certain is that it feels like a surprise party you suddenly remember you planned for yourself, that it is a profound sense of awe and delight, unceasing wonder, and a liberating and eternal disbelief. *Wow! I didn't believe this was possible!* These are the attributes of *who you really are* and the signs of awakening.

Belief in Who You Really Are

I will now ask you to do something in complete opposition to everything you've previously read in this book. I will now instruct you in the most forbidden and esoteric secret of all, one that I have kept hidden until now. I will now repudiate and deny everything I have already written and ask that you *believe.* Hold only one belief.

Believe only in yourself, your true self, that is, and the probability of your attaining it. Believe in this 100 percent, holding nothing back. Usually we hold back 50 percent or 10 percent or even 1 percent, deluding ourselves that we are giving it our "all." We are actually scared to death of what would really happen if we gambled completely and went for it without reservation. *All things are possible* if you put into action this belief, revolting against all limitations.

Have deep and abiding faith that it will all work out. If faith can move mountains of stone, it can surely move our small hills of flesh. At the flashpoint of 100 percent belief in self, miracles become commonplace and mundane. The universe will react to your wishes and your leg moves in unconscious response to your commands.

Politics is the Entertainment Branch of Industry.

—Frank Zappa

In a culture where approval/disapproval has become the predominant regulator of effort and position, and often the substitute for love, our personal freedoms are dissipated.

—Viola Spolin

This is not mystical mumbo jumbo but a very real law of our nature, and available to all, not just our mythological saviors, superhumans, or culture heroes. We have all had bone and spirit wrenching proof in our own lives that complete transformation and personal revolution are possible right here and right now, in this very instant. All our dreams can come true if we are brave enough to dream them and fearless enough to believe in them. Everything else is just lies.

It is pardonable when we spurn the proprieties, even the sanctities, making them stepping-stones to something higher.

—Henry David Thoreau

Who You Really Are and How to Get There

This book has insulted you long enough with its meaningless questions, vague hints, and rude proddings. This book, it seems, has taken its own advice all too well, and shaved the inside of its own skull and now has nothing to tell you about any of this. All this book can do is to describe our prison and furtively sketch a couple of risky escape routes. Once we've broken out, you're on your own and will most likely remember who you really were before your imprisonment and where your real home lies.

Your only crime is in not trying to free yourself. This book refuses to become another jailer. This book will repeat its author's all-time favorite story of the Zen Master who, when asked to describe the moon, simply pointed at it. All his students said, "Ahhh! The moon is a finger!" never once following his suggestion to look up at it for themselves. Says Lao-tzu, "Those who know, don't say. Those who say, don't know."

This book has said enough to now admit that it doesn't know what your freedom will feel like, what you will call it, or who you really are. It will, however, close this section with yet another Zen story and the best escape route that it knows of. Don't worry, the guards, interior and exterior, won't understand it at all. It's our secret.

A student asked a Zen Master where she could enter Zen. "Hear that brook?" he asked her.

"Yes," she replied.

"Enter there," he said.

Where can you re-enter your true self and become who you really are? Where are you as you read these words?

Enter there

Freedom is always against
the law.

•

—Church of the SubGenius

Fifth Set of RAZORS

Who we really are
is a constantly changing,
conscious and deliberate journey through life,
not an unmovable, frozen point of view.
Who we really are
is a process that can be unfrozen
only by revolting against everything
that conspires to tell us *who we are*
and who we're **supposed** to be.

The process of revolt
can be as innocuous as saying "Hello"
or as extreme as burning money.

Use this final set of razors to
revolt against who we're **supposed** to be,
who we're **told** to be,
and who we **think** we are.

Becoming yourself
is the most revolutionary act of all.

193

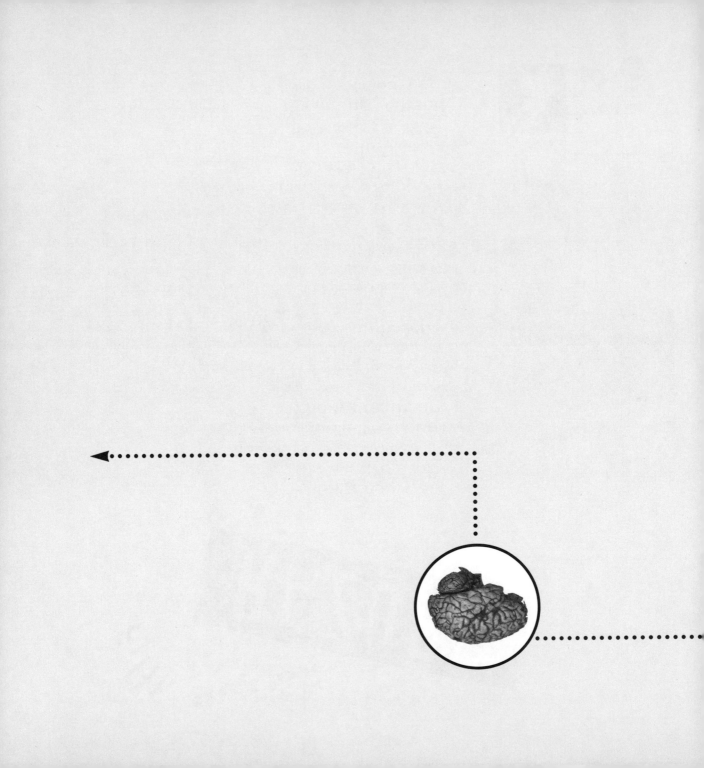

Burn Your Money!

There's a great picture of Abbie Hoffman burning money in front of the Stock Exchange and laughing like hell! In Alejandro Jodorowsky's film *The Holy Mountain*, seven diverse people are studying with a spiritual Master in an effort to attain truth and immortal life. As one of their last exercises, they are told to burn their money. It's interesting to watch the people's reaction and nearly physical pain as they push their money toward a fire-filled hole in the center of the table at which they're seated.

In our commodity culture, our sense of self and worth is tied to money, as well as our means of obtaining it. For one to question the power of money is more revolutionary these days than to question the power of God. Monetary atheism is more unforgiveable and unthinkable than the garden variety. It is, after all, called The Almighty Dollar! Burning money is an act of personal, economic, and spiritual revolt of an extreme sort.

So your razor is this: Burn your money! No, no, not all of it! After all, you need to buy more of my books! Just a dollar or so to see what it feels like and how much of a sense of nearly religious guilt you experience over this. To really feel blasphemous, spit on it first. To increase the amount of liberation and revolt from monetary beliefs (and guilt), increase the amount.

Burning money might actually be illegal in this country other than burning it in the socially approved fashions, so let's just pretend that this whole exercise is only a fantasy, not a real suggestion, OK? After all, you wouldn't want to break the law, would you?

Make a Mistake

Persian rug weavers, although capable of weaving a flawless carpet, would always insert one mistake. It was their feeling that to create something perfect would be blasphemous since "only Allah is perfect." In this way, they honored their higher power and kept "right size."

Try to do this whenever you're trying too hard to be "perfect." Insert a deliberate error to confirm your humanity as well as to revolt against the neurosis of perfectionism. Or if you discover an inadvertent error in your work or behavior, shrug, smile, and say, "Only Allah is perfect!" (This is, by the way, the *perfect* excuse for almost anything, although that is not the reason I put it in the book!)

Examine your beliefs about "perfection" and its neurotic and often blasphemous and idolatrous place in our lives. Here is the eror in this section as an example.

Revolt Against Old Superstitions

Superstitions are really just ancient beliefs that still haunt the most "enlightened" of us. Revolt against your superstitious behavior by: walking beneath a ladder, breaking a mirror, stepping on a crack, opening an umbrella inside the house, or allowing a black cat to walk in front of you.

If you have a personal, probably inherited, superstition, break it consciously. How did it feel?

Invent New Superstitions

The Surrealists invented their own new superstitions as means of assaulting "normal" reality and common beliefs. Some surrealist examples: Cupboards left open bring good luck. Wearing red socks on Wednesday will attract wealth.

Revolt against the common superstitions by inventing your own and behaving accordingly.

Share these new superstitions earnestly with others. Write

down at least two new superstitions of your own invention. Be careful. They could become beliefs of the far future!

• • • • Do Nothing!

Start by doing nothing for an hour. As you get more nonaccomplished at this, try to "do" nothing for a day.

The Taoists call this *wu wei,* that is, doing nothing; "nothing" being understood as a quite active verb. Sort of like "be-ing." Next time your beliefs want you to stop becoming who you are, say, "Nothing doing!" Revolt against the idea that we must always be doing something "productive." You're already doing it. Put this book down and do nothing for five minutes.

> The hardest work is to go idle.
>
> —Yiddish proverb

Create Idols •

Krishnamurti once said that you could place a stone on a table, maybe on a nice cloth, surround it with flowers, burn candles, offer it food, etc. Pretty soon, this would become an altar. Everyday, you could sit in front of it, reverently. Pretty soon it would be more than a stone and you would be less than a free person. The stone would own you.

We do this all the time, unthinkingly. We do it, of course, with religions and we do it as well with more abstract things like beliefs about self, world, and others.

The razor: Make a little altar and place something insignificant or even ridiculous on it, say a Barbie doll or a pack of gum. Observe the same rituals a person would who was in church or temple, bowing to it, burning incense, and whatever else you can do without laughing. At the end of the week, see if you can throw away the object of your veneration. Is there any difference between Jesus and Barbie, between Buddha and a pack of gum? Only in your mind and in the amount of attention and belief you invest. Creating ridiculous idols will cause a revolt in your mind against serious ones as well.

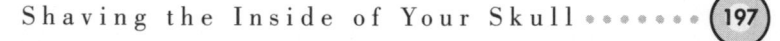

Destroy Idols

Is there some famous person you admire, respect, emulate, or revere? Someone you've placed on a mental altar? Get a picture of them. Tear it up. Throw it away. Revolt against membership in any form of mental fan club.

You can still admire the person after this razor. This is an exercise to test your resistance to destroying symbols and an indication of your willingness to make real your revolt.

A Zen story: One newly enlightened Zen student was found warming his hands over the burning wooden Buddha altar statue he'd thrown in the fireplace. He explained to the shocked monks that there being no wood, the statue was performing the highest act of compassion.

Question Authority, Part 1

Ask "why." We're constantly asked for personal information these days by people we don't even know. Asked for our zip codes at cash registers. Asked for our names by salespeople. Asked our opinions by pollsters. Asked for names of relatives on forms. Asked for amounts of ID that would make Soviet security blush. Asked for our annual income. Asked our names by anonymous telemarketers on phones. Most of us give the information automatically.

Ask back. Ask: Why do you need to know? Ask: Who wants to know? Ask them for *their* numbers. Why do this, you ask? Because it'll make you aware of how much we've surrendered of our personal privacy; because it's a simple act of revolt these days to simply ask, "Why?" The information monster insatiable and insensate. You don't have to feed it.

Ask! At the bank. To cops. To your clergy. To your parents. To your children. To the grocery clerk. At the post office. The evangelists at your door. The bellowing talk show host. Your politicians. Inquiring minds want to know.

It is only when the individual divorces themself from the rigors and regulations meant as psychological restrictions that true "ART" can be born.

—Lydia Lunch

Throw this book against the wall right now!

• • • • Did You Do It?

Did you throw this book? If you did, congratulations! You revolted against the book.

If you didn't, congratulations! You revolted against a written command!

If you threw it, how did it feel? Sacrilegious to throw a book? Silly?

If you didn't, why not?

Revolt Against Your Hands

If you're right-handed, use your left today, all day. Vice versa for you lefties. Our dominant hands (and brain sides) reinforce who we are. If all day is impractical, try it for at least a half an hour as you go about household tasks, such as writing, cooking, cleaning, and dressing. Use your nondominant hand to turn the pages as you read the remainder of this section.

Revolt Against Bigotry

Shut a bigot up at the same time. Not long ago, a guy I knew casually was at my house concerning some local civic matters. As the conversation turned from the formal agenda we had been discussing, he became more comfortable and began bantering. At some point, he said, in an offhanded manner, something like, "Oh, you know, those Jews . . ." and kept talking as though he had merely been discussing the weather or some other immutable fact of nature. I stopped him and he acted genuinely shocked that I wouldn't participate in his bigoted hallucination. "But you're not Jewish," he said, smiling one of those knowing and cloying "we're both regular guys

here" smiles that have led to so very much suffering. "But I am," I said angrily, rising from my seat. He appeared quite shaken and still maintained his denial, nervously asserting, "No, no, you're not."

"How can you tell? What does a Jew look and act like?" I asked loudly as I showed him the door. He looked genuinely shocked as though he'd never considered this before. I've had occasion to see him publicly since and he always gives me a nervous and suspicious look that I know is hiding his thoughts of "Mel's a Jew." As he does this, I feel, indeed, very Jewish. In many ways, we become and feel how others perceive us. We become who we allow ourselves to think we are.

I've also had occasion to do this routine at other times, claiming to be gay, Latino, or atheist or whatever else I can reasonably pass myself off as when confronted by a bigot. The same scenario always happens. Why do this?

First: You revolt against the murderously polite manners many of us have, not wishing to cause trouble and so on, confronting these belief cowards with a visible enemy and immediate and unexpected resistance. Doing this stretches the absolute limits of who you think you are.

Second: The bigot has their own beliefs completely challenged as to what people really are. I'm sure that this guy will be curbing his poisonous little tongue from now on, never quite sure just who it is he's talking with, no matter how well he believes he knows them.

Thirdly and most important: You get to actually feel what it feels like to be perceived as a member of these target groups and experience being treated as an object. Sounds like fun, doesn't it? Doing this, you absolutely revolt against who people assume you are. You also revolt against your own self-definition.

Say Hello to Strangers

Smile at them! Peel those eyes off the sidewalk and look at people! They actually smile back! When they do, it's like receiving a recharge of the spiritual batteries through your pupils. I know this is a very hard one to do or even to remember.

Although it seems pretty safe and mundane and may even sound trite and obvious, you're actually risking a lot of self-image, emotional armor, and beliefs about self and others. It's an act of revolt to be nice sometimes; revolting against impersonality. Also, the next time someone gives you the finger on the highway, blow them a kiss and smile. Who you really are is friendly.

Revolt Against Your Own Commands

Another surrealist exercise: Knock on the door, shout "Come in," and do not go in. Go do this right now.

Revolt Against Your Dreams

Pinch yourself at various times to make sure you're not dreaming.

Pinch yourself right now.

Revolting Fashion

Wear something outrageous, atypical, or out of character or something you really like, but you're afraid of what people will think. Do this even one time and you'll loosen up, become more yourself, and lose some of that old fear of not fitting in with whatever the current belief system is selling.

You might even discover that nobody gives a damn, anyway, and that it was all in your head (as usual). Apply this lesson to other areas of your life such as "fashions" in philosophy, politics, or whatever. It's all window dressing, really.

It's not only the emperor who has no clothes. Wear something "weird" or abnormal today.

Do Not Read This Sentence!

Backwards Read

This is an old proofreader's trick. In order to protect yourself from being hypnotized by text or brainwashed by seductive words, put the brake on your reading and throw the visual drive in reverse.

In this way, the buzzwords stand out more clearly from the background of text and you can view them as they really are: just words, not the thoughts in your head that they obligingly become. Revolt against what you're being told in print; deconstruct it with this exercise.

Your razor: Read the last two paragraphs backwards. I'll start you out: :out you start I'll. backwards paragraphs two last the read: razor Your.

Reading Between the Lines

This is a surrealist exercise by André Breton and Paul Eluard: "Do not read, look at the designs created by the white spaces between the words of several lines in a book and draw inspiration from them."

This is an excellent way to revolt against the written word and the tyranny of the trained eyes. Unfocus your eyes and gaze at this page, paying attention to the white space. Do this as well with trees, placing your attention on the shapes formed by their branches rather than the branches themselves.

What's not there is defined by what is there. What's not obviously there is often as important as what is there.

Just Say No!

John Lennon's "Working Class Hero" equates beliefs and consumption with drugs: "Keep you doped with religion and sex and T.V./And you think you're so clever and classless and free. . . ."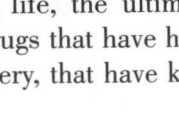

Examine the larger influences in your life, the ultimate pushers of the beliefs. These are the very real drugs that have hypnotized and addicted you into suffering and slavery, that have kept you from becoming who you really are.

Your razor: List and describe three beliefs in drug terms. Examples: Religions = Hallucinogen. T.V. = Valium. Politics = Thorazine. But list your drugs specifically, naming the brand you might consume, such as specific T.V. shows, variants of psychology, and so forth.

You will see that you are only as clever and classless and free as they will allow you to be. Revolt and detox right now!

How to Say No

"The Science of Advertising" was the heading of this revealing and juicy little secret revealed in a trade paper I happened upon. Unbelievable! These people are so brazen about their methods of mind control that they actually leave them lying around for any of us to see! The best part is that this little article was proud of this "science." So here for your own edification and liberation is their cute little "scientific" formula:

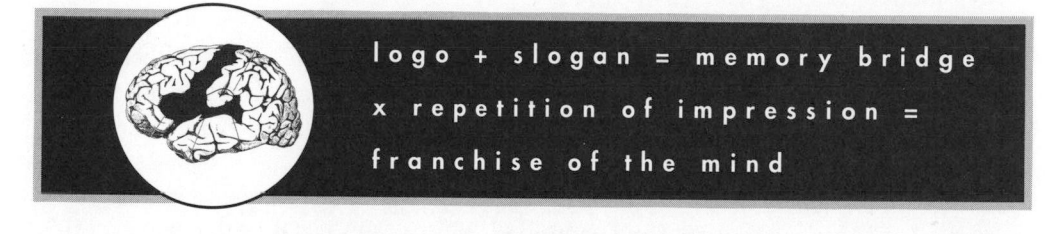

logo + slogan = memory bridge x repetition of impression = franchise of the mind

Your mind has been targeted as a franchise, like the shiny burger places and warehouse stores, like the ideologies and religions that flood the airwaves. Politicians, religious leaders, businessmen, all using this formula to actually own what you thought was yours: the stuff inside your skull. Are you free? Or free merely to choose between the packaging of product/belief A or B?

Your razor: Copy and tape this formula on your T.V. as you watch ads. Better yet, memorize it backwards as a modern spell to ward off the smiling franchisers of this twisted belief pyramid scheme.

Revolt against blatant brainwashing. A "franchise of the mind" is not who you really are. Reclaim your mind as an independent small business, a Mom & Pop consciousness operation rather than as a homogenized component of a belief and control distribution system.

•••• Name Names

Now that you have memorized the formula for the "Franchise of the Mind" and are fully in the control of this book, we'll proceed to naming the ways that your mind is purchased without your knowledge or consent: FEARS.

Fear is the coin which is used to control and addict you to beliefs and suppress your revolt. If you pay close and conscious attention to advertising, be it commercial, political, or religious, you'll soon notice that each can be deconstructed to a fear which is pressing your consumer button. The fear of standing out, of not standing out, of being unliked, of dying, of low status, of others, of condemnation, of whatever. The ads equate consumption of product/belief with happiness and freedom from fear.

Razors: Next time you watch T.V., read a magazine, or see a billboard and encounter an ad, name it out loud! Name it with the fear it is attempting to arise in your psyche. For print media you might write the fear's name in large, bold, even angry letters over the ad, article, or editorial.

This section of *Shaving the Inside of Your Skull* is appealing to your fear of being manipulated and controlled. Scrawl CONTROL with a pen over this part of the book.

Maybe being oneself is always an acquired taste.
—Patricia Hampl

Talk Like an Animal

Roooaaaaaahhhhrrrrgggggghhh! ARG!

Return to the roots of mammalian expression by roaring your emotion, ecstasy, and pain, cutting loose from limiting syllables and clever mental codes of control. Says Michael McClure in *Ghost Tantras,* "Poetry is a muscular principle and a revolution for the body-spirit and intellect and ear . . . To dim the senses and listen to

inner energies a-roar is sometimes called the religious experience." The book is written nearly entirely in "beast language" to be read aloud.

Let your muscles and bones and spirit roar, revolting against the limits of symbolic language. Try writing a paragraph in beast language and then roar it aloud, either alone or with others. "Who you really are" is in your muscles, mammal, not in heaven or hell or this or any book or word. Who you really are is the revolt of your body against cerebral ownership. Roar right now: JNAAAAHHHHGGRAMOOOOOOGGG!

Walk Like an Animal

Peter Elliot has created the "Animals Inside Out" workshops in London. In the workshops, people jump around and shout like animals, selecting an animal to imitate. Anything: an elephant, bat, condor, buffalo, monkey, moose, whatever. You are supposed to scratch, sniff, hang from trees, chew grass and twigs: whatever your particular animal does.

You could try this for a few minutes or more and see what happens. Reclaim your mammalian heritage. Are we really the highest animal? What kind of animal would you be, if you could be an animal?

Strike a blow for devolution, revolt against limiting human behavior, and act like the animal of your choice for a couple of uninhibited moments. Again, like many of the activities in this book, this is particularly fun and rewarding if done with others, especially children.

Question Authority, Part 2

Are you as sick as I am of telemarketers calling you at inconvenient times to sell you their crap? Or asking you personal questions just so they can add to their market targeting data bank? Even I will find myself answering them without thinking, volunteering information just because a disembodied electronic voice has broken into my home over the phone line.

We have become all too willing to surrender our privacy and rights over to any voice possessing the least artificial shred of authority. Later on I feel cheapened and used.

Ask *them* for *their* names. Ask them if they like their jobs. Ask them how they feel about bothering people. Ask them why, exactly, they need this information. If they won't cooperate, ask for their supervisor. Usually as this point, they'll disconnect and you can resume your dinner in peace.

You can do this as well with random surveys in the mall, the street, and so forth. Who wants to know and why? Refuse to cooperate in this madness. Declare yourself a sovereign nation of one and regard these people as very dangerous spies. Enjoy your dinner.

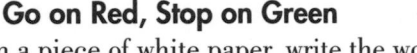
Don't play what's there, play what's not there.
—Miles Davis

Go on Red, Stop on Green

On a piece of white paper, write the word "Red," using a green crayon. Underneath it, write the word "Green," using a red crayon. Look at this for a while.

As well as learning that you shouldn't believe everything that you read, some odd psychological things will happen to you as well. Your brain will be nearly overwhelmed by the simple contradiction and you might even experience some resistance to doing this.

Your mind will revolt against accepting that "Green" is just a word, not a color. You must revolt against your limited mind and see the color of trees, not the grayness of words. Remember this exercise when confronted with definitive labels, be they religious, political, or economic. Reverse them in your mind in order to revolt and return to the real.

3½ Seconds to Freedom

I read that people look at billboards and ads for no more than 3.5 seconds at most. You would do well to pay closer attention to billboards all around you, dropping assumptions that you already know what they say or look like. You'll be really surprised at what you see! Maybe nothing really dramatic, but you'll see new things nonetheless, even from objects in your home that you believe you know intimately. You'll find that your beliefs about what you see don't match up too often with what's really there. Just *look* and pay attention without expectations.

An example: A billboard I've been seeing on the highway is advertising an expensive vehicle. Inside is what appears to be a happy, "normal" family. One day, I examined it a bit closer and realized that the family is featureless and literally resembles crash-test dummies. The billboard artist had counted on people's minds fleshing out his visual shorthand. Who are the real dummies here?

Your razor: Examine a billboard or visual advertisement you're already "familiar" with for at least ten seconds. Do you see anything different from what you expected?

Use your attention to revolt against your assumptions.

Stand Your Ground

Too busy to meditate, you say? Baloney! Remember how we used to think how lucky we were to live in Western society and not have to stand in long lines like those poor godless Russians? Those were the good old days. Now it's lines everywhere.

The razor: Say you're standing in a long bank line at noon on your lunch hour (this, of course, is the time that bank management decides to let the tellers go to lunch, too, leaving scores of angry people facing one teller in a positively Soviet-style bread line). Anyway, if the line so much as moves forward one tiny inch, everybody in line moves up that carpeted inch, even though they're really not getting any closer, just more packed together and upset.

Next time, don't move up that inch, but hold your ground. You'll get to the teller just as fast. Nonetheless, somebody will inevitably tell you that the line has moved up, urging you to do the same.

Instead, just pay attention to your breath, other people's reactions to the line, and your refusal to budge. Meditate, cool out. This time is an unsought-for gift from modern society. Be prepared, however, for the grumbles and whispered resentments of those behind you who in all honesty believe you're keeping them from reaching the teller.

You'll be revolting against herd behavior and using the time to become who you are. Grocery lines, gridlock traffic, ATM lines: the opportunities for a gentle revolt are endless!

> **Nice-ism** *n.* tendency, more or less socially codified, to approach reality in terms of whether others behave cordially; tyranny of decorum which disallows thinking or acting for oneself.
>
> —John Zerzan, *The Nihilist's Dictionary*

Resign!

Or: "Take this belief system and shove it; I ain't believing this no more!" Transcendentalist writer Henry David Thoreau would often write letters to the editor announcing his resignation from organizations and systems of thought to which he'd never belonged in the first place.

You, too, can try this by compiling a list of five public belief systems or organizations that you quit, although you may not believe or belong to them, anyway. This exercise will make real your refusal to cooperate in what the French called the "public hallucination."

Next make a list of five of your own beliefs that act as limits on your possibilities. Personally, I hereby resign from the belief that what I say can influence anyone; I resign from a belief that love doesn't last; I resign from a fear of failure. What are yours? Quit them! If so inclined, announce these resignations publicly. Pink slip that belief boss in your head!

The Nirvana Effect

This is a commonly observed syndrome found in people who read books such as this one or who attend "self-help" workshops. Also called "The Pink Cloud" in the Twelve Step programs, it takes the form of a giddy feeling that one's life has been changed for the better forever.

This feeling usually begins to dissipate within twenty-four hours, usually upon encountering minor irritations such as traffic or lines at the bank, which tend to drag the newly enlightened one down into the muck of icky everyday life. Usually, the book or workshop that originally inspired the "Nirvana Effect" is then bad-mouthed for not being a miracle worker.

A story: A monk meditated for years alone on a mountaintop, attaining perfect love. Wishing to share his insight, he returned to the crowded village below and was jostled before he could speak. He became so irritated that he punched the nearest passerby for interrupting his mission.

The razor: Set realistic goals and expectations for yourself. Attempt to identify just one, even seemingly minor, insight that you gain through any self-help activities. Any other way is no help at all. Maybe this very technique I've just outlined is the one you'll find most valuable in this entire book. I hope so. In fact, I know so.

List just one simple thing you've gotten from this book, one not subject to the "Nirvana Effect."

Your Own Razor

Write your own method of shaving the inside of your skull on the following lines. In this way, you've not only revolted against this book, but you've edited it yourself with your handwritten contribution.

_____

_____

_____

_____

_____

_____

_____

_____

_____

_____

If you feel it's appropriate, send it to me care of the publisher, with permission to reproduce it. If I use it, you'll get to see your name in print and receive a free copy of the book it appears in. But don't let that deter you.

Truth in Packaging

Somebody in one of my Shaving the Inside of Your Skull workshops told me to put this in the book, so here it is:

Today Is the Last Day of Your Life
How will you live it?

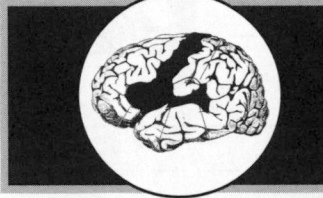

In case of starvation, you can eat this book. It's full of baloney.

The Final Razor

A paraphrase of Jack Kerouac: If you've understood this book, throw it away. If you can't understand this book, throw it away. I insist on your freedom.

Congratulations!

You have nearly completed *Shaving the Inside of Your Skull* (or at least reading a book with that title). In honor of your singular achieve-

ment, you are hereby entitled to put your name on this fine and authorized certificate, place it in a handsome frame, and display it proudly in your home, thereby winning the admiration and adulation of your family, neighbors, and friends! It might even win you promotions, pay raises, and T.V. appearances!

(sign your name here in fancy calligraphic script or mark with an X)

has read, understood & implemented the contents of

Shaving the Inside of Your Skull

Please extend all privileges and courtesies that attend to the above signed,
but don't believe anything they say,
especially about having actually read, understood and implemented this book.

SEAL

Date: _____

Mel SR

Official Signature of Author

READING RAZORS

Publishers and dates listed are from the editions I used. All of the suggested books are in print, or available in new editions from different publishers, or can be special-ordered at your local library.

Yes, the list is a rounding up of many of the usual suspects, but most of these works remain essential background material for shaving the inside of your skull.

First Shave

Emerson, Ralph Waldo. *Complete Essays.* New York: Modern Library, 1940.

Laing, R. D. *The Politics of Experience.* New York: Pantheon Books, 1967.

Modern Primitives. Re/Search. San Francisco, 1989.

Paine, Thomas. *The Age of Reason.* New York: Paine Foundation, 1952.

Thoreau, Henry David. *Walden.* New York: Bramhall House, 1961.

Watts, Alan. *The Book: On the Taboo Against Knowing Who You Are.* New York: Pantheon, 1966.

Welch, Lew. *Ring of Bone: Collected Poems.* San Francisco: Grey Fox Press, 1989.

Writing something
To leave behind
Is yet another kind of dream:
When I awake I know that
There will be no one to read it.

—Zen Master Ikkyu

Second Shave

Bateson, Mary Catherine. *Peripheral Visions.* New York: Harper Collins, 1994.

Bey, Hakim. *Immediatism.* San Francisco: AK Press, 1994.

Burroughs, William S. *The Adding Machine: Selected Essays.* New York: Arcade, 1993.

Debord, Guy. *The Society of the Spectacle.* New York: Zone Books, 1994.

Jeffrey, Francis, and John C. Lilly. *John Lilly, so far . . .* Los Angeles: Jeremy P. Tarcher, Inc., 1990.

Lilly, John C. *The Center of the Cyclone.* New York: Bantam, 1972.

McLuhan, Marshall. *Understanding Media.* New York: Mentor, 1964.

Roszak, Theodore. *The Cult of Information.* New York: Pantheon Books, 1986.

For it is written that nothing is written.

—Jesse Sump, Epistle to the Dallasasians

Third Shave

Ferguson, Marilyn. *The Aquarian Conspiracy.* Los Angeles: Jeremy P. Tarcher, Inc., 1980.

Hoffer, Eric. *The True Believer.* New York: Time, Inc., 1963.

Krishnamurti, J. *Freedom from the Known.* New York: Harper & Row, 1969.

Leonard, George B. *The Transformation.* Los Angeles: Jeremy P. Tarcher, Inc., 1981.

Maslow, Abraham. *Toward a Psychology of Being.* New York: Van Nostrand Reinhold Co., 1968.

Murphy, Michael. *The Future of the Body.* Los Angeles: Jeremy P. Tarcher, Inc., 1992.

Reich, Charles A. *The Greening of America.* New York: Random House, 1970.

Roszak, Theodore. *The Voice of the Earth.* New York: Touchstone, 1992.

Sagan, Carl. *Dragons of Eden.* New York: Ballantine Books, 1978.

Fourth Shave

Ash, Mel. *The Zen of Recovery.* Los Angeles: Jeremy P. Tarcher/Perigee, 1993.

Buber, Martin. *Hasidism and Modern Man.* New York: Harper, 1958.

Clarke, Arthur C. *Childhood's End.* New York: Del Ray, 1981.

Leary, Timothy. *The Politics of Ecstasy.* New York: G. P. Putnam's Sons, 1968.

McKenna, Terence. *The Archaic Revival.* New York: HarperCollins, 1991.

Ouspensky, P. *The Psychology of Man's Possible Evolution.* New York: Vintage Books, 1974.

Vonnegut, Kurt. *Cat's Cradle.* New York: Holt, Rinehart and Winston, 1963.

Watts, Alan. *Beyond Theology: The Art of Godmanship.* New York: Vintage Books, 1973.

Weiner, Herbert. *9½ Mystics: The Kabbala Today.* New York: Collier Books, 1992.

The point of these teachings is to control your own mind: Use only as directed.

—Stephen Billias, The American Book of the Dead

Fifth Shave

Bey, Hakim. *T.A.Z.* New York: Autonomedia, 1991.

Charters, Ann. *The Portable Beat Reader.* New York: Penguin Books, 1992.

Hoffman, Abbie. *The Best of Abbie Hoffman.* New York: Four Walls Eight Windows, 1990.

Leary, Timothy. *Chaos and Cyberculture.* Berkeley: Ronin Publishing, 1994.

Marcuse, Herbert. *One-Dimensional Man.* Boston: Beacon Press, 1969.

McClure, Michael. *Lighting the Corners: On Art, Nature and the Visionary.* Albuquerque: University of New Mexico Press, 1994.

SubGenius Foundation. *The Book of the SubGenius.* New York: Fireside Books, 1987.

Vaneigem, Raoul. *The Revolution of Everyday Life.* San Francisco: AK Press, 1992.

Wilson, Robert Anton. *Cosmic Trigger II.* Scottsdale, Az.: New Falcon Publications, 1991.

Yatri. *Unknown Man: The Mysterious Birth of a New Species.* New York: Fireside, 1988.

Zappa, Frank, and Peter Occhiogrosso. *The Real Frank Zappa Book.* New York: Poseidon Press, 1989.

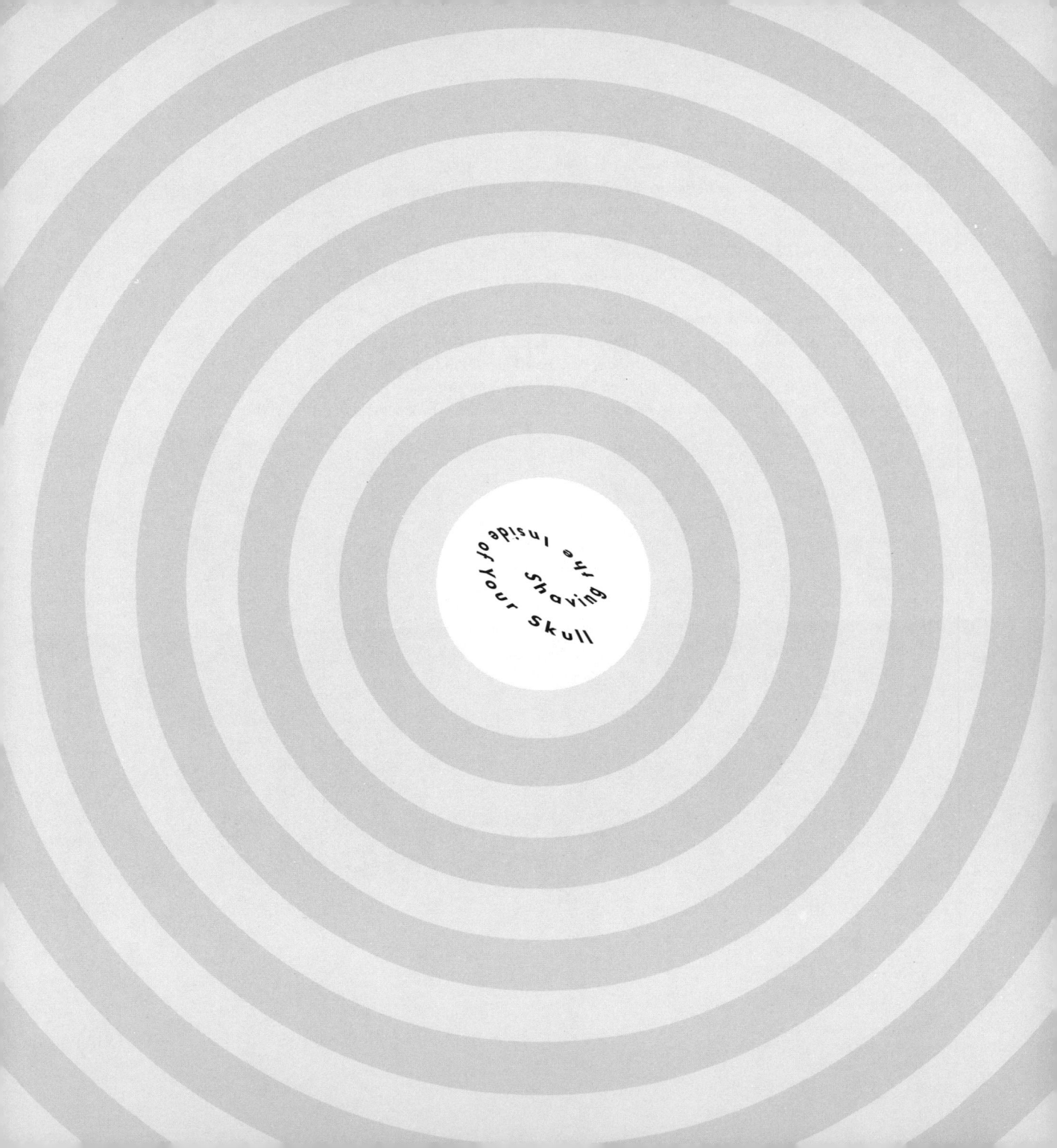

THE TWO COMMANDMENTS
OF BELIEF

(ACCORDING TO <u>SHAVING THE INSIDE OF YOUR SKULL</u>)

I

THOU SHALT BELIEVE

THE SECOND COMMANDMENT

II

THOU SHALT NOT BELIEVE

THE FIRST COMMANDMENT

Mel Ash is a writer, artist, and teacher/performer with a lifelong interest in transformative experience, cultural change, and consciousness. A former authorized Zen teacher in an Asian tradition, he has taught workshops nationally on Zen, Beat spirituality, and alternative psychology.

Present during many cultural shifts, he attended Woodstock as a young teenager, worked at a punk rock paper in the eighties, and is currently active in contemporary alt. culture, exploring the cultural dimensions of spiritual action.

In addition to *Shaving the Inside of Your Skull*, he is also the author and illustrator of *The Zen of Recovery* (1993) and the forthcoming *Beat Spirit* (both published by Tarcher Putnam). He is currently researching and working on his new book *Zaddik*.

He is active in Providence's First Unitarian Church, lives with Sarah Owens-Ash, a Boston radio personality, his two sons, many cats, one newt, and occasional wayfarers in Providence's "International Neighborhood."